David F. O'Connell, PhD
Deborah Bevvino, PhD, CRNP

Managing Your Recovery from Addiction

A Guide for Executives, Senior Managers, and Other Professionals

Pre-publication
REVIEWS,
COMMENTARIES,
EVALUATIONS . . .

"This book offers both proven and practical strategies to staying sober as well as deep inspiration and a vision of hope and happiness for business professionals. Our patients have found it a very useful tool."

Don Serratt, CEO
Life Works Treatment Centre,
London, England

"*Managing Your Recovery from Addiction* is the indispensable resource for every person in a position of responsibility confronting a problem of substance abuse because it uses the abuser's career skills to create success in recovery. The book uses terms familiar to any professional, such as strategy, conflict management, organizational behavior, and sidestepping the issues to bring the abuser's skill set to rehabilitation."

Jay Glaser, MD
www.AyurvedaMed.com

Managing Your Recovery from Addiction

A Guide for Executives, Senior Managers, and Other Professionals

HAWORTH Addictions Treatment
F. Bruce Carruth, PhD
Senior Editor

Neuro-Linguistic Programming in Alcoholism Treatment edited by Chelly M. Sterman

Cocaine Solutions: Help for Cocaine Abusers and Their Families by Jennifer Rice-Licare and Katherine Delaney-McLoughlin

Preschoolers and Substance Abuse: Strategies for Prevention and Intervention by Pedro J. Lecca and Thomas D. Watts

Chemical Dependency and Antisocial Personality Disorder: Psychotherapy and Assessment Strategies by Gary G. Forrest

Substance Abuse and Physical Disability edited by Allen W. Heinemann

Addiction in Human Development: Developmental Perspectives on Addiction and Recovery by Jacqueline Wallen

Addictions Treatment for Older Adults: Evaluation of an Innovative Client-Centered Approach by Kathryn Graham, Sarah J. Saunders, Margaret C. Flower, Carol Birchmore Timney, Marilyn White-Campbell, and Anne Zeidman Pietropaolo

Group Psychotherapy with Addicted Populations: An Integration of Twelve-Step and Psychodynamic Theory, Second Edition by Philip J. Flores

Addiction Intervention: Strategies to Motivate Treatment-Seeking Behavior edited by Robert K. White and Deborah George Wright

Assessment and Treatment of the DWI Offender by Alan A. Cavaiola and Charles Wuth

Countertransference in Chemical Dependency Counseling by Gary G. Forrest

Solutions for the "Treatment Resistant" Addicted Client: Therapeutic Techniques for Engaging Challenging Clients by Nicholas A. Roes

Shame, Guilt, and Alcoholism: Treatment Issues in Clinical Practice, Second Edition by Ronald T. Potter-Effron

Treating Co-Occurring Disorders: A Handbook for Mental Health and Substance Abuse Professionals by Edward L. Hendrickson, Marilyn Strauss Schmal, and Sharon C. Ekleberry

Designing, Implementing, and Managing Treatment Services for Individuals with Co-Occurring Mental Health and Substance Use Disorders: Blueprints for Action by Edward L. Hendrickson

Federal Narcotics Laws and the War on Drugs: Money Down a Rat Hole by Thomas C. Rowe

Managing Your Recovery from Addiction: A Guide for Executives, Senior Managers, and Other Professionals by David F. O'Connell and Deborah Bevvino

Managing Your Recovery from Addiction

A Guide for Executives, Senior Managers, and Other Professionals

David F. O'Connell, PhD
Deborah Bevvino, PhD, CRNP

The Haworth Press
New York

For more information on this book or to order, visit
http://www.haworthpress.com/store/product.asp?sku=5485

or call 1-800-HAWORTH (800-429-6784) in the United States and Canada
or (607) 722-5857 outside the United States and Canada

or contact orders@HaworthPress.com

PUBLISHER'S NOTE

The development, preparation, and publication of this work has been undertaken with great care. However, the Publisher, employees, editors, and agents of The Haworth Press are not responsible for any errors contained herein or for consequences that may ensue from use of materials or information contained in this work. The Haworth Press is committed to the dissemination of ideas and information according to the highest standards of intellectual freedom and the free exchange of ideas. Statements made and opinions expressed in this publication do not necessarily reflect the views of the Publisher, Directors, management, or staff of The Haworth Press, Inc., or an endorsement by them.

Identities and circumstances of individuals discussed in this book have been changed to protect confidentiality.

The Twelve Steps are reprinted with permission of Alcoholics Anonymous World Services, Inc. (AAWS). Permission to reprint the Twelve Steps does not mean that AAWS has reviewed or approved the contents of this publication, or that AAWS necessarily agrees with the views expressed herein. A.A. is a program of recovery from alcoholism *only*—use of the Twelve Steps in connection with programs and activities which are patterned after A.A., but which address other problems, or in any other non-A.A./ context, does not imply otherwise.

This book has been published solely for educational purposes and is not intended to substitute for the medical advice of a treating physician. Medicine is an ever-changing science. As new research and clinical experience broaden our knowledge, changes in treatment may be required. Although many potential treatment options are given herein, some or all of the options may not be applicable to a particular individual. Therefore, the author, editor, and publisher do not accept responsibility in the event of negative consequences incurred as a result of the information presented in this book. We do not claim that this information is necessarily accurate by the rigid scientific and regulatory standards applied for medical treatment. **No warranty, expressed or implied, is furnished with respect to the material contained in this book. The reader is urged to consult with his/her personal physician with respect to the treatment of any medical condition.**

Cover design by Jennifer M. Gaska.
TR: 3.6.07

Library of Congress Cataloging-in-Publication Data

O'Connell, David F.
    Managing your recovery from addiction : a guide for executives, senior managers, and other professionals / David O'Connell, Deborah Bevvino.
        p. cm.
    Includes bibliographical references.
    ISBN: 978-0-7890-2739-9 (hard : alk. paper)
    ISBN: 978-0-7890-2740-5 (soft : alk. paper)
    1. Professional employees—Substance abuse. 2. Executives—Substance abuse. 3. Substance abuse—Patients—Rehabilitation. 4. Management. I. Bevvino, Deborah. II. Title.
RC564.5.P76O36 2007
362.29068—dc22
                                                                            2006031214

CONTENTS

Preface

Addiction, as the saying goes, is an equal-opportunity destroyer. It can affect anyone regardless of race, ethnic background, socioeconomic status, occupation, or station in life. Yet not all chemically dependent individuals are the same. Addictions treatment professionals have realized this for years, and they have tailored addictions treatment to a patient's unique personality, needs, life circumstances, gender, and age. Executives and professionals have special needs and require an addictions treatment approach that targets these needs and problems.

Executives and professionals are found to be highly motivated, successful, often competitive, and usually very driven. Typically, they have a great deal of responsibility in their careers, and professions. They are often very independent, self-reliant, and highly intelligent. In addition, they are often demanding and critical, and possess finely honed interpersonal, problem-solving, and organizational skills that have served them well in the workplace. However, these same qualities, strengths, and skills associated with occupational and financial success can contribute to and perpetuate an addictive disorder. It is our experience that identifying, intervening with, and treating an executive with an addictive disease can be challenging and complex.

The executive individual's self-image typically disallows identifying with the stereotype of an alcoholic or addict. This perceptual bias can strengthen the denial and other defenses that are operative in an addictive disorder. Executive patients are often very intelligent, powerful, and resourceful and function well even during a serious addiction. They can continue to handle a large volume of work and do it very well, often to the amazement of co-workers and supervisors alike. Again, this can contribute to denial of an addictive disorder

Managing Your Recovery from Addiction
© 2007 by The Haworth Press, Inc. All rights reserved.
doi:10.1300/5485_a

vii

since the executive patient appears to be doing so well. However, as the disease of addiction progresses, executives who are chemically dependent know they are not meeting their own often exceedingly high standards. Although workplace functioning is usually the last thing to be affected, in the later stages of addiction, the deleterious effects of this chronic, insidious disease are apparent.

The good news, however, is that with proper treatment and an investment in recovery, all of the qualities, traits, and behaviors of the executive/professional can be used in pursuing sobriety. These characteristics can propel the patient to new heights of happiness and well-being in recovery. Executive and professional patients are highly motivated to pursue recovery. After all, they have much to lose. Research has shown that 85 to 90 percent of executives are successful in recovery if they are given appropriate treatment and adhere to a treatment plan in ongoing recovery guidelines. This statistic is far higher than for the general population.

This book is based on clinical experience of treating professionals and executives, psychological theories of behavior, and models of addictions treatment and was designed to help lay the foundation for the professional's continued recovery. We have found that most executives and professionals take on large amounts of responsibility, such as driving a corporation's missions, health, and effectiveness; caring for the lives and health of others; executing government policy; and securing funds and conducting rigorous research. Many are in highly visible positions in entertainment.

Typically, executives and professionals are in leadership positions, are in charge, and call the shots. They execute and/or oversee how others carry out a particular work decision as well as develop and operationalize plans, objectives, strategies, and ideas. Many have been immensely successful, and others look up to them as role models.

Corporations and institutions invest much in grooming the talent of the executive. The executive individual is among the most important resources and powerful competitive weapons in the marketplace. Executives need constant attention and care, and smart organizations take care of their executives. We have found that executives typically do very poorly with self-care. Executives and professionals take on the burdens of leadership but often lack ability to nurture and take care of themselves. This is particularly true of the chemically dependent executive. Teaching executive patients to work a selfish program in recovery, to challenge those beliefs and attitudes that block them from taking care of themselves, and to plunge them into a life of self-care and self-nurturance is paramount.

It Is Hard to Get You into Treatment!

Detection of illness is another challenge in the treatment of the executive. It is difficult to detect and confront addicted behavior in individuals who are in leadership positions, especially within a corporation. After all, who is going to confront the boss? In the work environment, people are worried about their jobs. Because of the executive's power and influence, few people are going to confront even the most obvious addicted behaviors. The executive is therefore insulated from detection and intervention because of his or her own power and position.

The financial compensation associated with being in upper management also provides insulation against detection of an addictive disease. If you have a lot of money, you can buy a lot of cocaine, alcohol, heroin, or other drugs. It is harder to "hit bottom" in the addictive process when you are gainfully employed and financially well off. Therefore, an executive can continue addictive behaviors much longer than someone without the same resources.

Executives also have a great deal of scheduling flexibility and freedom. They do not have to punch a time clock and can disappear for long periods of drinking and drugging. Moreover, executives are often engaged in informal socializing with clients and customers, which frequently involves heavy alcohol consumption. When they are off drinking or drugging, nobody is checking to see whether they are at their desks. Often it is assumed they are off on important business.

Likewise, it is often extremely difficult to detect job deterioration with the impaired addicted executive. The executive's job description is more abstract and less well defined than the job descriptions of those in lower positions within the corporation's hierarchy. Much of the executive's effectiveness depends on such "soft" commodities as problem-solving skills, interpersonal skills, social intelligence, strategic thinking, planning abilities, and vision. Because these skill sets are more difficult to define and assess, an executive can typically do less and less in the work environment without being held accountable. This is termed *job shrinkage*. That is, the executive continues to perform at a high level but actually engages in fewer and fewer tasks.

The Emotional Health of the Addicted Executive

In our experience many executive individuals are unhappy. They are in a psychological dilemma. Early in life, the future executive learned that recognition and validation often accompanied some type of achievement, usually athletic or academic. After all, everybody loves a winner. The executive patient developed a compulsion to succeed and excel. He or she became driven at an early age. Many executives come from families where love was conditional. Love, attention, and affection were bestowed upon the future executive based on the young child's successes in the classroom or in athletics. The unfortunate lesson learned by the young future executive was that it is not what you are but what you do that counts.

Many executives come from dysfunctional, often alcoholic households. They eventually took on the "family hero" role and obsessively pursued advancement and achievement to compensate for the devastating effects of alcoholism on themselves and their family. However, the effects of alcoholism are not so easily brushed aside. Lingering, gnawing, and deep feelings of inadequacy, insecurity, and inferiority may accompany the executive into adulthood and are only partially assuaged by the spoils of success. A lack of self-love and self-esteem can be temporarily offset by achievements; however, this solution is almost always futile. It simply does not work. Deep down inside we all know that more power, more money, more sex, more pleasure, and more prestige cannot substitute for the love of self. However, most of us do not know how to deal with this dilemma. The executive's solution was to become driven and competitive in order to achieve and thus to overcome a sense of inadequacy. The cost of this strategy, however, is a chronic feeling of being a fraud. Addicted executives secretly harbor a fear that they do not deserve their successes. They are at odds with themselves. They have difficulty opening up to others and being intimate because they fear that others will eventually see through them and detect their inner insecurities and unhappiness. This primal fear of being discovered to be a fraud can lead to even higher levels of drivenness and compulsive behaviors. Eventually, the executive feels more and more alienated and lonely, and advancement and achievement can come to substitute for genuine, healthy, open, intimate relationships with others.

Executives often develop a false sense of self or persona. They develop strong defenses against feelings of inadequacy, insecurity, and pain by developing a type of mask. To others they may come across as positive, upbeat, secure, confident, optimistic, in control, capable, and in charge. In fact, this is the type of persona that we all make want to project in the workplace. However, the executive is in danger of "becoming" his or her persona; the true self is lost or hidden. Such individuals can become cut off from their genuine feelings, impulses, and desires. They become similar to a character in a play. Because this style of functioning minimizes pain and contributes to success, it is extremely seductive and the executive becomes locked into a form of false existence. What is happening on the outside stands in marked contrast to the immense pain being experienced on the inside.

An executive's life can become one of avoidance: avoidance of inner pain and discomfort through powerful psychological defenses and distracting behaviors. Among these behaviors is excessive work or work addiction. Compulsive work is an effective way to avoid many things in life: intimacy, conflict, inner discomfort, inadequacy, and stress. Another mechanism of avoidance is perfectionism. This orientation to life is based on obsessive, illusory control. Perfectionism bestows a sense of safety, predictability, and security. It comes at a high cost, however. Perfectionist individuals never enjoy the fruits of their labors because as soon as a task is completed, another goal or project immediately takes its place. The perfectionist individual is unable or unwilling to celebrate his or her successes. Perfectionism covers over deep feelings of grief, loneliness, isolation, and fear. There is often an obsessive future orientation to life. The present moment somehow does not count. With perfectionism it is all about controlling some perceived future event to acquire some imagined outcome. Perfectionists place unrealistic, irrational, often cruel demands upon thmeselves and others. They are critical of others who do not subscribe to the same personal standards. Inwardly the perfectionist resists these demands and expectations and is angry about this self-imposed predicament, but he or she rarely confronts it, and even more rarely develops an exit strategy to acquire psychological freedom and well-being.

Executives also often have other addictions and compulsions. These can be diseases in their own right, but they also serve to distract and to deflect the addicted executive's attention from dealing with his or her addictive disease. Such behaviors include pathological gambling, sex addiction, spending addiction, and food addiction.

The Addicted Male Executive

It is useful to look at what we know from research and clinical experience about the alcoholic male executive. According to research, in a moderate-size company of, say, 5,000 employees, the probability is that 15 of the approximately 250 top executives in the company are alcoholic or drug addicted. Other studies suggest that 10 percent of highly placed executives are drug or alcohol impaired. The overwhelming majority of executives today are male. They function within a subculture that is based upon traditional male values. Among the main distinctions between an alcohol-dependent executive and other chemically dependent men is the broad, pervasive impact that the executive's addictive illness has on the lives of others. Executive alcoholism, regardless of the size of the company, has a wide-ranging, devastating effect on the corporation and beyond.

Male executives struggle to portray a certain image. The qualities traditionally associated with male executive positions are strength, clarity, decisiveness, endurance, competence, and a highly competitive orientation. Men with these qualities are afforded respect and status in American society. They are viewed as leaders and as authorities. Consequently, such an individual is less likely to be challenged when his abuse of alcohol and drugs becomes problematic. The secure, powerful, authoritative male executive may seem invulnerable to the ravages of addiction. After all, he is in control of his life. How could his use of alcohol be out of control? The male executive also has power and is expected to accomplish difficult tasks and to achieve success against the odds. Male executives are expected to have the capacity to adapt, to bring about change, and to control events to ensure successful outcomes. Corporate leaders assume that a male executive who is abusing alcohol or chemicals will be able to change himself. He is expected to have the willpower to control alcohol or drug use and to perform well for the company. This is, of course, a false perception, a myth.

The Chemically Dependent Female Executive

Executive women in treatment present a distinct set of dynamics. First, they are often survivors and achievers, learning to flourish in a competitive, task-oriented, male-dominated business climate. Moreover, these women are involved in multiple roles: parent, spouse, caretaker. Most women who are employed outside of the home report increased self-esteem and social support, despite their increased responsibility and performance demands. Typically, a woman struggling to meet the demands of a job and raising a family does not show any adverse impact on mental health or increased drinking behavior. However, research has shown that increased drinking among working women is correlated with their level of employment and type of work. For example, women working in male-dominated occupations are more likely to report increased drinking or adverse consequences of drinking. It has been reported that high-ranking women executives are more likely to be heavy drinkers than women of comparable age and education who are employed in lower-level jobs. Some researchers believe that heavier drinking patterns among employed women are influenced by factors such as greater access to alcohol and complex issues surrounding delicate gender balance and dynamics in the workplace or occupation. In addition, the literature indicates that women are influenced by their need for a connection to their male peers and may be imitating the male drinking model (fitting into the good-old-boy network). Executive women may see drinking behavior as symbolic of an expression of power and gender equality. Indeed, successful high-achieving executive women often have to deal with resentment, envy, high performance expectations, loneliness, alienation, and stressful occupational demands placed on them. Many executive women are inwardly ambivalent about their success because they may expect negative consequences from it, such as social rejection, feeling unfeminine, and feeling socially isolated. They also have to contend with society's ambivalence about women acquiring, maintaining, and exerting power and influence in the workplace.

Some high-achieving women have dealt with these dilemmas by attempting to feminize the workplace. They foster a less competitive and more collaborative, cooperative work environment with an emphasis on interdependence among its corporate members. Many high-achieving women executives leave successful corporate positions to create their own feminized workplaces through entrepreneurial pursuits. Such women, more likely than not, find creating their own psychological work climate more gratifying than attempting to adhere to the status quo of a male-dominated workplace.

Psychological research has identified some troubling inner conflicts for executive women. Some executive women are inwardly fearful of becoming too successful and powerful. At a deeper level they may fear surpassing their own mothers, whom they often viewed as weak and confined by the traditional female role. Many such women come from families with alcoholic fathers with whom they experienced a greater identification than they did with their own mothers, whom they saw as deficient. They often emulate their fathers and may feel more comfortable relating to men than to women. They may have difficulty with the maternal role. They become extremely self-reliant and independent and have trouble accepting any needs for dependency. They may have difficulty with nurturing behavior. Many women remain unmarried and become workaholics. They feel isolated in the workplace and alienated from female friends who may have chosen a more traditional, domestic life.

The Repercussions of Executive Addiction

As you may have experienced, an untreated active alcoholic executive can have a devastating impact on the organization he or she serves. Addiction compromises the executive's capacity to provide direction, guidance, and leadership within an organization. As the disease progresses, the executive's behavior can become more erratic and inconsistent, compromising his or her decision making and judgment. The executive becomes more and more emotionally absent, and often physically absent as the addiction process leads to greater and greater deterioration. Even so, the addicted executive often rallies and has periods when things seem to go very well. He or she may perform excellently on a specific project. On a good day, the executive can project an image of authority and power. This unfortunately strengthens the denial and leads to a false sense of confidence in those around the executive. As the executive's addiction progresses, coordination is lost between various divisions within a company. The clarity of objectives and goals diminishes, conflict and confusion can escalate, and the company can lose focus. As these problems become evident, those in the organization frantically focus on the external business environment or internal issues within the company and rarely identify and deal with the obvious problem: the executive's alcoholism or drug addiction. People scramble to look for a quick fix to solve complex, systemic problems within the organization that are the direct result of executive alcoholism.

Eventually, the impact on the ultimate indicator of corporate well-being, the financial bottom line, becomes obvious. The corporate culture in the workplace unfortunately works against confronting addiction, and circumstances continue to deteriorate. Those around the executive alcoholic may make excuses for him or her, cover up for missed appointments, justify the executive's mistakes, and explain away irrational behavior by attributing problems in the company to other causes. Everybody knows that something is wrong, but rarely is it attributed directly to the executive's drug addiction. Nobody wants to be the whistle-blower. Research studies show that more than 75 percent of newly sober executives reported that their secretaries and administrative assistants conducted elaborate cover-up operations to camouflage their drinking. Sixty percent of newly recovering executives say that their fellow executives protected them while they were drinking. Ninety percent of formerly alcoholic executives say that they found it necessary to come in early, stay late, or work on weekends to compensate for their diminished ability to get work done effectively within normal time frames.

Early Recovery and This Book

So now you have learned something of what clinicians know about executive-level addiction. We hope this information gives you an even greater insight into the dynamics surrounding executive-level addiction and firms your commitment to staying sober. It is our hope that this book will help you navigate through early recovery.

A Message to the Reader

The starting point for your journey in recovery was your inpatient treatment experience. There, the central knowledge, skills, and strategies to establish you on the path to sobriety were learned. The components of sobriety were presented in a supportive, nurturing, trusting, and loving psychological climate and environment. In this type of environment you were free to let down your defenses, experience your own vulnerability, disclose you innermost secrets, and gain a strong sense of intimacy with yourself and others. For many of you that was an unprecedented time in your life; perhaps the first time you became completely honest and open with yourself and others. You learned about the effects of alcohol and other drugs of abuse on the brain and body and learned the dynamics and characteristics of addictive diseases. Some of you may have passed through the phase of withdrawal and attained physiological stability and regained your health. If treatment was effective and useful, you were able to establish the foundation for your recovery and learn a blueprint for getting and staying sober.

Now that you are out of the inpatient environment and back in your life again, the journey of recovery continues. A new set of challenges now confronts you. The challenge now is to sustain the changes and progress you attained during your inpatient treatment. You now need to establish continuity in your life by meeting the demands of early recovery.

The process of recovery, we know, is a developmental one. Success builds gradually, incrementally, and cumulatively. With each day of abstinence your mind and body become stronger, more flexible, and more adaptive. Each day in recovery you learn something new. The real world is upon you now. Daily conflicts, power struggles, and the

Managing Your Recovery from Addiction
© 2007 by The Haworth Press, Inc. All rights reserved.
doi:10.1300/5485_b   *xvii*

demands of family and work life make your commitment to an intact recovery program challenging. You begin to deal with the day-to-day stresses of life and emerge triumphant over them without drinking or drug use, yet in the back of your mind you are concerned about relapse into active addiction. Knowing that maintaining abstinence and sobriety is the prerequisite for success in your life from now on, you are adjusting to a life without the effects of alcohol and drugs. New aspects of your mental and emotional life begin to emerge and you are reclaiming your psychological and spiritual life. Perhaps for the first time in your life you are learning and experiencing the true meaning of good health and well-being. We hope that this process excites you.

This workbook was designed to help you as an executive/professional meet the demands and challenges of maintaining your recovery program in the first year of the recovery process. The book is divided into seven lessons structured and focused around developing a strategic recovery plan. As you well know, it is axiomatic in the business world that proper planning improves performance. In devising your strategic plan, you will extend the successful blueprint you developed in your inpatient care. You will learn to "plan your work and work your plan." In addition, you will learn the vital knowledge and approaches to maintain recovery, prevent relapse, and manage relapse if it occurs. Also, a lesson on understanding and managing conflict is included that will help you in your personal, family, and work life. Managing conflict, arguments, and associated upsetting emotions can be a major challenge because alcohol and drugs no longer are used to assuage painful feelings. Related to this, a long section on spiritual development in recovery offers both academic and practical information. Cultivating a rewarding spiritual life that facilitates and enhances your recovery is paramount. A section on managing feelings and moods in recovery is also included. Relapse research shows that painful emotional and mood states are the chief cause of a return to active addiction. The information and strategies presented in this lesson can help you maintain a balanced and fulfilling emotional life. Finally, the book concludes with a summary lesson on essential recovery knowledge processes that you can return to periodically to consolidate and strengthen your recovery program.

We congratulate you on completing your intensive inpatient experience and committing yourself to lifelong recovery. The intention of this book is to guide you in the first year of recovery and we trust that it will be useful to you.

ABOUT THE AUTHORS

David F. O'Connell, PhD, is attending psychologist for the executive/professionals program at the Caron Treatment Centers and Lifeworks of London, England, an internationally recognized addictions treatment facility, where he was formerly the clinical director. He serves on the consulting staff of the Department of Psychiatry of the Reading Hospital & Medical Center. Dr. O'Connell developed the first executive treatment program at Lifeworks Addictions Treatment Center in London, and is a trainer for Chrysalis in County Wicklow, Ireland. He is a member of the American Psychological Association, Division on Psychopharmacology.

Dr. O'Connell received his doctorate in organizational development from Temple University in Philadelphia, and has done postdoctoral study in clinical psychopharmacology at Farleigh Dickinson University in New Jersey. He is listed in the National Register of Health Service Providers in Psychology. Dr. O'Connell is the author/editor of six books, including *Self-Recovery: Treating Addictions Using Transcendental Meditation and Maharishi Ayur-Veda* (Harrington Park Press), and is an expert on holistic, alternative approaches to addictions recovery and spiritual development.

Deborah Bevvino, PhD, CRNP, is Coordinator of Behavioral Medicine and Faculty Associate at the Family Practice Residency Program and staff Psychologist at the Reading Hospital and Medical Center, Reading, Pennsylvania. She is an adjunct faculty member in the Department of Family Medicine at Temple University and is a board-certified adult nurse practitioner. She has practiced in the area of women's health and addiction medicine. Dr. Bevvino is a consulting psychologist at the Caron Treatment Center, Wernersville, Pennsylvania, where her practice focuses on women's addiction treatment in extended care.

Dr. Bevvino has extensive teaching experience in medical, nursing, and psychology education and as has presented at regional, national, and international conferences. Her research interests are in the area of post-traumatic growth, addiction in women, and medical education.

Lesson 1

Creating and Implementing a Strategic Recovery Plan

INTRODUCTION

Businessmen and women, as well as other professionals involved in management, know the value of planning in addressing business problems. Management involves planning and guiding one's efforts to achieve some desired goal. Both the function of management in general, and strategic planning in particular, can be applied to the development and maintenance of recovery from an addictive disease. From our perspective, the same knowledge and skills that have been developed in your occupational life can be applied to the management of your recovery and the development of lifelong sobriety.

The process of management generally involves a number of functions, including planning, anticipating, strategizing, problem solving, evaluating, organizing, monitoring, influencing, and maintaining. These functions are also important in the development and maintenance of sobriety. Although you cannot directly control the expression, manifestation, and nature of your addictive illness, you can take responsibility for managing your recovery and the processes that facilitate remission of the disease and achieving maximum physical and mental health in recovery. Management skills, knowledge, and tasks all have the purpose of helping you achieve a desired goal—in this case sobriety. Tasks such as planning, goal setting, decision making, and communicating all have a role to play in the maintenance of sobriety. We believe that the maintenance of sobriety occurs

Managing Your Recovery from Addiction
© 2007 by The Haworth Press, Inc. All rights reserved.
doi:10.1300/5485_01

one day at a time. Putting this objective into operation involves management tasks and skills.

Look at how certain management tasks can apply to the recovery process:

- *Planning* is involved when, for example, you structure your day to include prayer and meditation, attendance at an AA meeting, and a meeting with your sponsor, and when you structure your daily activities to minimize stress and to maximize personal satisfaction.
- *Goal setting* is also implicit in managing recovery. You no doubt have the overarching goal of lifelong abstinence and sobriety one day at a time. This is actually a good example of effective goal setting. This goal is specific, measurable, and has a time frame. This and other goals you may have in recovery can guide all of your daily efforts and decisions.
- *Decision making* is another vital management function that can be utilized in the service of recovery. Good decision making involves a six-step process:

  1. Defining the problem
  2. Gathering information about it
  3. Analyzing the information
  4. Developing options to deal with the problem
  5. Choosing and using the best option
  6. Monitoring the outcome and the success of the option you chose to address the problem

It is clear how sound, effective decision making is important in recovery, just as in the business world. For example, say you have to attend a business function early in recovery that involves alcohol use among colleagues and customers. You may define this as a problem. If it is, you first gather information:

- Who will be in attendance at this gathering?
- Is it absolutely essential that you have to be there?
- How long will it last?
- Will any expectations to drink be placed upon you?
- What will be the dynamics of this social/business gathering?
- How will it impact on your job?

Next, you analyze the information so you can clearly see the potential threat to your sobriety and develop options to deal with the problem. For example, you may decide to avoid the meeting entirely, or you may want to reduce anticipated social awkwardness by coming up with a rationale for your not drinking, such as a medical problem. You might stay at the meeting a brief time and then excuse yourself. After looking at these options, you choose the best one and implement it.

The next step is for you to monitor the outcome:

- How well did you handle the situation?
- How much internal discomfort did you have?
- Did it trigger any urges to drink or use drugs?
- It is a situation you can handle again with a minimal amount of discomfort and inconvenience?
- Did it seem to have an appreciable effect on your business and personal relationships?

This is just one simple example of how the management skills you have honed over the years can be used in the service of managing recovery. Of interest is the fact that physicians and other health care providers are beginning to apply these same management principles and strategies to the treatment of the full spectrum of diseases. This is an area known as *disease management.*

Other concepts involved in management are useful in understanding and carrying out recovery plans. For example, managers are interested in the value they create for customers. For a recovering individual, it is important to keep the value of recovery in mind. Continuous recovery from addictive diseases is a prerequisite for happiness and quality of life. Nothing has greater value than abstinence and sobriety for a chemically dependent individual. Profitability is another concern for a manager. In our case, it is important to think of personal profit. A life free from the bondage of addiction is indeed a profitable life. It is important to keep in mind the many advantages and benefits of sobriety. The sober individual has the opportunity for good physical and mental health, happiness, and greater freedom in life. "The sky is the limit." Conversely, the costs of a return to active addiction are immeasurably high. Remember what you learned in inpatient treatment:

untreated addiction inevitably leads to total incapacitation, incarceration, or death. Managing recovery involves a continual appreciation of both the benefits of recovery and the costs of active addiction.

Managers are also concerned with performance. Performance is enhanced through proper planning. Proper and effective planning in recovery can help recovering individuals perform recovery maintenance tasks regularly and effectively. Performance involves execution of recovery maintenance tasks and strategies. There is a saying in business: "Plan your work and work your plan." If you have solid goals and objectives and you are mindful of executing recovery maintenance strategies and recovery tasks with subsequent monitoring and evaluation of your performance, you significantly enhance your chances of lifelong recovery.

Communication is another vital management task. It is important to communicate your needs and concerns to others during recovery and likewise to develop good listening skills, particularly in the twelve-step meetings, in groups, and in individual counseling sessions. Using some basic communication skills such as "I" statements and active listening skills are paramount to ward off potential emotional discomfort.

A good manager is also aware of his or her own limitations and the resources available in the environment. Sometimes it is important to outsource, to reach out to others who have vital skills and knowledge that can help you maintain recovery. Reaching out to others and securing necessary help and resources is often difficult for recovering professionals. Knowing when you need help, knowing how to ask for it, and developing the confidence to execute the process is crucial.

GOAL SETTING IN RECOVERY

Determining your recovery goals is an easy process. Keeping them in mind on a daily basis and using them to guide your daily affairs is more difficult. Writing your goals down and referring to them daily keeps you more focused on achieving them. In this section, you will determine your recovery goals in five areas:

- Physical/medical
- Psychological/emotional
- Spiritual

- Social
- Occupational/work

Determining Your Physical/Medical Goals

As you learned in inpatient care, taking care of the body is extremely important, especially during the first year of recovery. The neurotoxic effects of drug and alcohol abuse can linger for months after the initial treatment experience. Because of this you need, first and foremost, regular and deep rest. Obviously, you also need proper nutrition, regular exercise, and dynamic activity to keep your life in balance. You really need to avoid acquiring deep fatigue. This means that you should not overwork, that you should get to bed early, and in general that you should have a good, regular daily routine. The first year of recovery is about the stabilizing and purifying effects of abstinence.

Studies on the neurological and cognitive effects of addiction clearly show that most neuropsychological damage incurred during active addiction is at least 80 percent reversible during the first year of abstinence. After that, the benefits of complete abstinence level off. Clearly, in the first year of recovery you should do everything physically possible to stay abstinent and avoid relapse to active addiction.

The following are examples of goals and strategies for physical health in recovery:

Physical Goals	Achievement Strategies
• I will avoid becoming deeply fatigued.	I will get eight to ten hours of sleep per night. I will take regular breaks during the day at work. I will work no more than forty hours per week.
• I will achieve optimal physical health.	I will exercise for at least one half-hour three times per week. I will take vitamins and other nutritional supplements. I will see my doctor for medical monitoring every three months. I will eat a balanced diet.

In Worksheet 1.1 list your physical recovery goals and fill in your ideas on achievement strategies.

Psychological/Emotional Recovery Goals

You learned in inpatient treatment that the regular use of alcohol and psychoactive drugs of abuse leads to emotional mismanagement and can also lead to severe problems with mood. Addicts in active addiction regularly feel extreme anxiety, fear, depression, despair, grief, shame, guilt, and other negative emotions. The neurotoxic effects of alcohol and drugs on the nervous system directly cause much of the emotional turmoil associated with addiction. With abstinence and rest as well as proper therapy many of these emotional and mood problems resolve without difficulty during the first few months of recovery. It is therefore important to be aware of your emotional health. Setting goals to manage your emotions and moods can prevent emotional mismanagement, subsequent mental suffering, and possible relapse or return to active addiction. In general, substance abusers are at greater risk for the development of depression, anxiety disorders, and other psychiatric disorders than the general population. You should be particularly alert to problems such as a severe drop in mood or a regular feeling of anxiety and nervousness. If you have any questions about problems with your emotions and moods, you should see your family doctor, a psychiatrist, or a clinical psychologist.

You should be particularly aware of the development of the disorders of depression and anxiety.

Depression

Depression usually has emotional, physical, and mental symptoms. A persistent low mood or feeling of deep sadness or the blues marks depression, which may also involve feelings of deep guilt, irritability, agitation, and frustration. On the mental level you may become very indecisive, lose interest in life, and become extremely self-critical, which leads to poor self-image and feelings of inferiority or inadequacy. Physically you may experience sleep pattern changes, such as an inability to fall asleep or early morning awakening. You may also notice a deep drop in libido or sex drive. You may lose your appetite.

WORKSHEET 1.1. Your Physical Recovery Goals

In the following spaces list your physical recovery goals and fill in your ideas on achievement strategies.

Goals	Achievement Strategies

1.

2.

3.

4.

5.

You may become preoccupied with health concerns. As depression progresses suicidal thoughts and impulses may become evident.

Anxiety

Anxiety disorders affect 15 percent of the population and approximately 25 percent of chemically dependent individuals. The disorders involve anxious feelings, anxious thoughts, and physical manifestations of anxiety such as tightness in the chest, rapid breathing, butterflies or discomfort in the stomach, restlessness, muscle tension, trembling, shaking, racing heartbeat, headaches, fatigue, hot and cold flashes, and feelings of rubbery or jelly legs. The emotional component of anxiety includes nervousness, worry, fear, feeling strange and unreal, feeling detached from your environment or your body, panic, apprehension, a sense of impending doom, and feeling stressed. Anxious thoughts include difficulty concentrating, racing thoughts, frightening fantasies, recurrent worries and fears, concerns about medical illness or dying, intense self-consciousness, and fears of being alone or abandoned.

Both anxiety and depressive disorders are treatable, and most respond to appropriate medications and psychotherapy or counseling. If you show any of these symptoms for more than a few weeks in recovery you should seek medical and psychiatric help.

In general, emotions and feelings that trouble chemically dependent persons in recovery do not reach the intensity and proportion of psychiatric disorders. Most recovering individuals struggle with the same emotions as everyone else. For example, feelings of grief, sadness, anger, frustration, jealousy, inadequacy, and guilt may exist. These feelings will tend to come and go in recovery and their presence should be accepted and tolerated. Learning to tolerate ups and downs in feelings and moods is an important developmental recovery task. However, if you find that a particular state or mood is beginning to dominate your functioning, then it is clearly time to do something about it. For example, walking around feeling angry all day at work and when you return home is definitely a danger sign and requires attention. Left unattended, destructive and dysfunctional moods and feelings can spin out of control and lead back to active addiction.

As you learned during your inpatient treatment care and through attendance at twelve-step meetings, personality problems or character defects can interfere with recovery, stop you from working your recovery program, and block you from being open to help, guidance, and assistance from others. Therefore, it is important to explore personality and character problems. Being mindful of them and taking steps to lessen their effects on your day-to-day behavior in recovery is important.

Ongoing Assessment of Attitudes, Beliefs, Traits, and Behaviors

In the executive/professional treatment program, awareness of dysfunctional maladaptive attitudes, beliefs, traits, and behaviors is important as the patient lays the foundation for recovery. In strategic recovery planning, it is important to make a good assessment of such attitudes and character traits. The O'Connell Dysfunctional Attitude Survey (see appendix) was developed to measure strengths and weaknesses in several areas: validation, achievement, affective (emotional) control, perfectionism, egocentricity, and drive. This survey was developed for executive professionals and managers in recovery. The results of this survey can be used to construct your psychological/ emotional goals in recovery planning. As indicated in the survey instructions, you can return to this test periodically throughout your first year of recovery to measure how your attitudes are changing over time. Alternatively, you can review these six domains of functioning by rating yourself on the survey provided in Worksheet 1.2.

After reviewing your progress along these dimensions, you can use your measurements in developing your psychological/emotional goals and achievement strategies. Remember, your personality is not etched in stone. As recovery unfolds, you may experience a great deal of inner psychological change that can be reflected in your outer behavior. As your spiritual program removes character defects and you continue to work a recovery program, you can expect that your attitudes, beliefs, traits, and behaviors will become less maladaptive and dysfunctional and more adaptive and evolutionary.

WORKSHEET 1.2. The Six Domains of Functioning

1. Validation

Problems with validation indicate that you place undue emphasis on others' opinions of you. This puts you in a dependent position and you are excessively judgmental and self-critical. Your self-esteem and moods are directly tied to whether you are getting the approval you desire from others. If this area is not problematic, you tend to enjoy your accomplishments for their own sake and you do not place so much emphasis on being admired and praised.

Current Rating (circle one):

1	2	3	4	5	6	7	8	9	10
LOW				MODERATE				HIGH	

2. Achievement

Problems with achievement indicate your self-esteem and well-being are intimately tied to your productivity and accomplishments. A high score is associated with workaholics. You deal with an inner sense of emptiness or lack by overachieving. You set unrealistic expectations and you push yourself constantly. A low score indicates that you are not bothered by this problem. You tend to feel gentified and you enjoy your achievements for their own sake.

Current Rating (circle one):

1	2	3	4	5	6	7	8	9	10
LOW				MODERATE				HIGH	

3. Affective Control

A high score indicates you tend to suppress, repress, or avoid emotions. You have difficulty with intimacy. You equate emotional expression with being vulnerable. You struggle to control your emotions. A low score indicates you tend to be emotionally free and spontaneous and that you are comfortable with yourself. You tend to be self-accepting and you do not view your intellect and reasoning abilities as so much more important than your emotions or intuitive capacities.

Current Rating (circle one):

1	2	3	4	5	6	7	8	9	10
LOW				MODERATE				HIGH	

(continued)

4. Perfectionism

This is another important area to review periodically. If you find yourself becoming too demanding both with yourself and with others, easily frustrated, impatient, critical, and angry, you are probably manifesting overly perfectionist behaviors. Watch out for becoming preoccupied with fears of failure. Perfectionism means that you may drive yourself at an intense pace and you feel little or no satisfaction when your goals are achieved. As soon as one of your goals is met, another one pops up and takes its place. Perfectionism is running high when you feel life is joyless and tedious. Your demands and personal standards are becoming unrealistic and impossible to carry out. The yardstick that you are using to measure performance is inappropriate.

Current Rating (circle one):

1	2	3	4	5	6	7	8	9	10
LOW				MODERATE				HIGH	

5. Egocentricity

If this area is problematic, you have a narrow, constricted view of life and you are at the center of it. You may feel a constant sense of frustration or irritability because your needs are not being met. When problems arise in your work or personal life, you personalize them and take too much responsibility for them. It is difficult for you to understand the perspective of others. You feel a sense of entitlement. A low score indicates that you are flexible and adaptable in dealing with life's disappointments. You are tolerant with yourself and others. When something goes wrong you do not automatically assume that you are the cause of it.

Current Rating (circle one):

1	2	3	4	5	6	7	8	9	10
LOW				MODERATE				HIGH	

6. Drive

If this area is a problem, you continue to have the sense that you have a lot to prove in your life. You show a lot of compulsive behaviors and become obsessed with any task that you are involved in—even to

(continued)

(continued)

the point of neglecting your health. You may be drawn to high-risk activities and novel experiences. You are constantly on the move and easily bored with routine and maintenance tasks. If this is not a problem, you tend to have a balanced approach to activities. You can enjoy silence and down time. You do not feel compelled or impelled. You enjoy your work and leisure activities in the company of others. You do not have to be constantly doing something.

Current Rating (circle one):

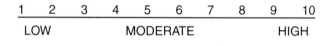

1	2	3	4	5	6	7	8	9	10
LOW				MODERATE				HIGH	

The following are examples of psychological/emotional goals and achievement strategies:

Psychological Goals	Achievement Strategies
• As much as possible, I will maintain a healthy balanced mood.	Repeat the serenity prayer daily. Work the Twelve Steps. Perform a moral inventory on a regular basis. Forgive others and myself as often as I can.
• I will eliminate perfectionism.	I will identify perfectionist behaviors when they arise. I will stop repressing and avoiding feelings behind perfectionism such as anger, grief, a fear. I will make time to have fun everyday. I will try to enjoy one moment at a time and forget about projecting into the future.

In Worksheet 1.3 list your psychological recovery goals and fill in your ideas on achievement strategies.

WORKSHEET 1.3. Your Psychological Recovery Goals

In the following spaces list your psychological recovery goals and fill in your ideas on achievement strategies.

Goals	Achievement Strategies

1.

2.

3.

4.

5.

Spiritual Recovery Goals

Remember that, first and foremost, the Twelve-Steps of AA are a spiritual program. Working a spiritual program leads to surrender, release, acceptance, and finally freedom and serenity. More than 1,000 studies have been conducted on the positive physical and mental benefits of engaging in spiritual technologies such as meditation and prayer on a regular basis. Some of these research results are compelling. For example, one study showed that individuals who practice transcendental meditation on a regular basis show a 50 percent reduction in doctor office visits and a 75 percent reduction in hospitalizations (Johnson, 1987). Studies on prayer where patients are being treated for coronary problems and cancer show significantly greater recovery rates for individuals who pray on a regular basis than for those who do not pray. Regular meditation and prayer can normalize blood pressure, reduce atherosclerosis, and eliminate mood problems such as anxiety and depression. Regular meditation and prayer lead to a state of equanimity and serenity and help the recovering individual develop knowledge to the level of wisdom.

Sobriety and recovery should be about freedom, and spiritual practices are an effective means to achieve inner freedom. This important research indicates that definite neurophysiological changes take place in the brain when one engages in meditation and prayer regularly. We are now beginning to understand the neurophysiological substrate of spiritual experiences and the spiritual awakening. The spiritual awakening as mentioned in the Twelve Steps has become a neuropsychological reality that can be measured by neuroradial techniques such as CT (computed tomography) and PET (position emission tomography) scans.

For the recovering addict, it is important to pray, meditate, and contemplate on a daily basis. This helps accelerate the growth of higher states of consciousness and helps cultivate deeper states of serenity and inner freedom. Regular prayer and meditation cultivates love and compassion, both for the self and for others. Studies also show that spirituality is good for business: employees who are involved in a regular meditation program, for example, show higher levels of productivity, effectiveness, and efficiency on the job and a greater sense of well-being in the work environment.

The following are examples of a spiritual goal and achievement strategies in recovery:

Spiritual Goal	**Achievement Strategies**
• I will make spirituality a priority in my recovery.	I will begin and end each day reading a prayer. I will learn and practice meditation for fifteen to twenty minutes, twice a day. I will schedule spiritual retreats twice yearly. I will read spiritual recovery literature on a daily basis.

In Worksheet 1.4 list your spiritual goals and fill in your ideas on achievement strategies.

Social Recovery Goals

Scientific research on relapse shows that after dysfunctional mood states such as anxiety and depression, interpersonal and social stressors are the next most frequent risk for relapse to active addiction. Clearly, both inpatient addictions treatment and ongoing recovery are social processes. We need other people to help us get and stay sober. Executive and professional patients need to overcome their extreme self-reliance and independence and reach out to others. Other people have knowledge, insights, and skills that we do not have. It is important to surround yourself with supportive, understanding people in recovery. Conversely, others, including family members, spouses, co-workers, and friends, can be a source of great distress in recovery. Conflict with others is inevitable. Our friends and family members can hurt us and let us down. They can humiliate us and can withdraw their love and affection. Because of this, developing the capacity to manage conflict when it occurs in interpersonal situations is crucial, as conflict is a setup for relapse. You could anticipate and even expect hurt and conflict in intimate relationships and not personalize it. It is true that you always hurt the one you love, and it is equally true that the one you love will hurt you. The secret to managing conflicts is listening, communicating clearly, negotiating, and compromising. When

WORKSHEET 1.4. Your Spiritual Recovery Goals

In the following spaces list your spiritual recovery goals and fill in your ideas on achievement strategies.

Goals	Achievement Strategies
1.	
2.	
3.	
4.	
5.	

you have a conflict with another individual, it is important to talk to them about the conflict. Do not withdraw or ignore the conflict. It will only worsen. Likewise, do not get locked into rage or anger. It may be easy to justify these feelings, but this will not help resolve the conflict. Define conflicts as mutual problems to be worked on and resolved. Resist the tendency to see conflict with others as win–lose situations. Always describe your feelings when you are involved in a conflict situation. This is a vital skill that you may have learned in inpatient addictions recovery. Telling someone how you honestly feel (such as "I feel hurt when . . .") in a conflict situation can have a magical effect in terms of bringing the conflict to a resolution.

In general, it is necessary to become realistic about our expectations with others in intimate and friendship relationships. Let go of the idea that people are here to meet your needs and live up to your expectations. They are not. It is not a universal law that individuals you love have to love you in return. Likewise, people do not have to appreciate you. Examine your life. How many relationships in your life have come and gone? The social context in which you are engaged in recovery will constantly shift and move. Recognize this and accept it. Do not give up on relationships unless they are a negative influence in your life. In many ways, good relationships are all we have in life. As much as you can, surround yourself with loving, caring, respectful individuals, and play this role with others when you can. The twelfth step also lets us know that it is important to invest in life by investing in the recovery of others. Whatever you acquire in recovery, you should be ready to give it away. After all, this was instrumental in your own sobriety.

The following are examples of social goals in recovery:

Social Recovery Goals	**Achievement Strategies**
• I will develop a solid support system in recovery.	I will meet with my sponsor or call him/her on a weekly basis. I will establish a home group in AA/NA. I will keep regular contact with trusted friends. I will attend regular social functions for recovering individuals.

- I will reduce the level of conflict I have with others at work.

I will let go of grudges I have with others.

I will seek to make amends to others I have wronged at work.

I will build collaborative relation ships with others at work that I have ignored.

I will become a mentor to another individual at work.

I will practice conflict resolution skills on a daily basis at work.

Please fill in your own social recovery goals in Worksheet 1.5.

Work Recovery Goals

For the recovering executive/professional patient, work should be about balance and satisfaction. Optimally, you should love what you do for a living. At the minimum, you should get at least some enjoyment from it. If you do not, you should seriously look for another line of work. In general, executives work too long and too hard. Remember your scores on the dysfunctional attitude survey. You may be a driven, approval-seeking, achievement-focused individual who is a perfectionist and controlling. Work can become a compulsion, an activity at which you are compelled to excel. As most working adults spend the majority of their non sleeping hours at work, it is important for the serenity and peace of mind achieved in sobriety to penetrate your work life. During recovery, you may have to reengineer your job to make it more recovery-friendly. You may need to set limitations on your work behaviors to avoid excessive work or work addiction. You may need to reset your goals and make your expectations at work more realistic, in line with your energy and abilities. As executives, you need to be constantly aware of problematic traits and behaviors such as intense achievement- and approval-seeking behaviors, and you may need to take steps to counterbalance these influences so that your work and professional life do not get out of control.

WORKSHEET 1.5. Your Social Recovery Goals

In the following spaces list your social recovery goals and fill in your ideas on achievement strategies.

Goals	Achievement Strategies

1.

2.

3.

4.

5.

If you have been diagnosed with work addiction, get treatment for it. You need to develop healthy relationships at work. If you spend too much time in isolation, then you need to reach out to others in your field or line of work to combat alienation. Conversely, if your workplace is intensely social, then you need time for yourself to meditate and to destress. If your financial goals and how you define financial success are taking too much of a toll on you or putting you at risk for relapse, then you need to reconfigure and restructure your ideas along different lines. The achievement of success should not mean the loss of your sobriety. You need to develop the mindset and the skills to adapt to continual, rapid change in the workplace. When possible, you should eliminate ambiguity at work. Have a clear understanding of the parameters and goals of your job, and guidelines for performance evaluation to assist in greater job satisfaction. Do not let overwork be a rationalization for not working your recovery program. In the long run, if you do not work a recovery program, then most likely you will no longer have a job.

The following is an example of a work recovery goal and achievement strategies:

Work Recovery Goal	Achievement Strategies
• I will establish a balanced work life.	I will work no more than forty-five hours per week.
	When possible, I will not take work home with me.
	I will take several breaks during the day for meditation, spirituality, and destressing.
	I will discuss the nature of my workload with my supervisor.
	I will develop time management and organization skills.

In Worksheet 1.6, fill in your work recovery goals and achievement strategies.

WORKSHEET 1.6. Your Work Recovery Goals

In the following spaces list your work recovery goals and fill in your ideas on achievement strategies.

Goals	Achievement Strategies
1.	
2.	
3.	
4.	
5.	

ANALYZING YOUR ENVIRONMENT
AND PERSONAL CIRCUMSTANCES

Following the construction of goals, the next step in strategic planning involves an analysis of the environment in which your recovery is taking place. Basically, you want to identify both threats to your sobriety and opportunities to enhance recovery. Becoming circumspect about situations and forces or circumstances that could dismantle your recovery program will prevent relapse. In addition, it helps to be vigilant about the opportunities present in your environment to help solidify and promote recovery. Threats to recovery could include particular conflicts you have with family members, friends, or business associates. Threats can include social situations that pose a high risk for returning to drinking or drug using. You should also analyze your interpersonal relationships and be especially aware of dysfunctional or destructive relationships.

Opportunities for recovery enhancement are everywhere, in many forms such as self-help books, relationships workshops, self-awareness exercises, and spiritual retreats that will give you the opportunity for in-depth spiritual experiences and personal development. Be particularly aware of individuals you meet in the course of your work or personal time who possess the wisdom and knowledge to help you accelerate your growth in recovery.

In Worksheet 1.7, brainstorm what you see as potential threats to your recovery and what you see as potential opportunities to enhance your functioning in recovery.

Once your recovery goals and situational analysis have been completed, the next step in strategic planning is to assess what you have going for yourself, your personal resources. These include your talents, skills, personality, strengths, relationships, positive habits, fund of knowledge, and physical capabilities. Keeping your own strengths and resources in mind will help you tackle recovery tasks more efficiently and effectively. In addition, knowledge of your limitations can help guide your efforts to enhance your recovery management skills and tools.

Brainstorm all those qualities and characteristics you possess that help you meet the challenges of life. Perhaps you have a sharp intellect. You may have finely honed organizational skills or wonderful

WORKSHEET 1.7. Threats and Opportunities in Recovery

In the following spaces list potential threats to your recovery goals and potential opportunities to enchance your functioning in recovery.

Threats to Recovery	Opportunities for Recovery Enhancement
1.	1.
2.	2.
3.	3.
4.	4.
5.	5.

personal daily habits that support health (such as exercising), practicing stress-reduction methods, and eating a balanced diet. Other examples are an excellent support system to help you cope during times of distress, computer skills that could help you access information and assistance if you get into trouble in recovery, and a solid religious upbringing that will be of use in cultivating spirituality and serenity in your sobriety program. Following your impatient treatment you may have developed a high capacity for introspection and self-awareness that will help you with problem identification and in combating denial, delusion, and other addictive defenses that may recur during early recovery. Finally, you may possess a strong physical constitution that has served you well during periods of illness and has helped you weather the deleterious effects of alcoholism and other chemical dependencies. It is important to be mindful of your personal resources and strengths so that you can draw upon them in your continued recovery.

In Worksheet 1.8, brainstorm as many of you strengths and resources as will contribute to the maintenance and enhancement of recovery from addictions.

DEVELOPING ACTION STEPS

Now that you have identified your goals, assessed the threats to your recovery and the opportunities for growth, and articulated your personal resources, you are in a position to expand upon the achievement strategies you briefly listed in the section on goal setting. However, ideas and good intentions alone are not enough to enable you to stay sober. Reading all the books we want on recovery, attending all the lectures on the disease model of addiction, and developing the most elegant, well-thought-out plans for recovery development will not make for continued recovery. It is daily action during recovery that is essential for meeting recovery goals. Action steps are therefore necessary to move you toward your recovery goals, neutralize or eliminate threats to recovery, capitalize on opportunities, and help you take advantage of personal resources you have in developing or maintaining sobriety.

In Worksheet 1.9 write out in paragraph form the action steps you will take in the five areas listed previously for goal setting (physical/

WORKSHEET 1.8. Assessing Personal Resources

In the following spaces brainstorm about your strengths and resources that will contribute to the maintenance and enhancement of recovery from addictions.

1.

2.

3.

4.

5.

6.

7.

8.

9.

10.

WORKSHEET 1.9. Action Steps

In the following spaces, outline the action steps you will take in the various recovery areas/dimensions listed.

Physical/Medical

Psychological/Emotional

Social

Spiritual

Work/Professional

medical, psychological/emotional, spiritual, social, and work/professional). Be as specific and complete as possible. The following is an example of developing action steps for spiritual development in recovery:

> I am going to develop a daily program for cultivating spiritual development; I am going to purchase several books on meditation and spirituality from the Hazelden Foundation; I will spend five to ten minutes each morning reading spiritual recovery literature; I will resume going to mass at least one Sunday a month; at work, I am going to take two breaks a day to practice meditation; I am going to attend a local transcendental meditation center to learn to practice meditation properly; I will spend at least one week a year on a spiritual retreat; I will attend a weekend workshop on directed and guided prayer; each night before I go to bed, I will review my day's activities and spend three to five minutes in silent prayer before retiring; I will go down to Borders bookstore and study the books on tape and books they have on various spiritual topics; I will commit to reading a new book on spirituality once every six months; I will develop a renewed interest in my religion by talking to the priest at my local parish; I will become involved in volunteer charitable activities at my church.

Writing down your action steps in this fashion will help keep them a live in your mind and will help you work your plan of recovery on a daily basis. Once they are written down, you can refer to them regularly.

IMPLEMENTING YOUR STRATEGIC PLAN

If you are in a business, you probably know that many businesses develop strategic plans only to ignore them and never implement them. However, you cannot afford to do this when it comes to recovery from addictive diseases. Addiction is, after all, cunning, baffling, and powerful. Too many internal and external forces are at work that would dismantle your recovery program. You have to plan your work and work your plan. It is also useful to share your plan with your spouse or other individuals with whom you are intimate. The more people know what you are trying to achieve, the greater the chance you will get support. If you find you are having difficulty with implementing the plan you developed, perhaps it needs to be re-engineered. It may be unrealistic for you. You may have to prioritize various areas of your strategic plan for recovery. Nobody can do it all, all the time!

Another obstacle to implementation may be that planning and carrying out activities in a structured way is foreign to you. You are being asked to develop a lifelong daily habit, and that is immensely difficult for many people. You may feel that your life is too complex or too busy to develop a plan and implement it. But remember, the more complex your life is, the more you need a simple plan. The more your life changes, the more you need an anchor and a rudder to help guide the change. A well-thought-out plan will help save time; it will make you more efficient. If you are bucking or avoiding developing and implementing a strategic plan for recovery, then this is an important issue to explore. It can be a manifestation of resistance. Recovery-based denial can rear its head in early recovery. As time passes after your initial inpatient treatment, it is easy to forget the lessons you learned in inpatient recovery and the pain you suffered due to active addiction.

MONITORING PROGRESS

Periodically, once per month, you should sit down with your strategic recovery plan and review your efforts. You can do this individually or with your therapist or sponsor. If your plan is too ambitious or unwieldy, you can scale back. Maybe your plan is not stretching enough and you have become bored with it. You can then enhance and expand it. As you grow in recovery, your goals will change and your recovery maintenance strategies will likewise change. Problems will resolve and will need to be replaced by new ones, that require different strategies and different ways of thinking about them. The point is that recovery is a lifelong process. You do not arrive one day at the state of sobriety.

Subjectively rating your progress against your recovery plan is a useful activity. In Worksheet 1.10, again write down your major recovery goals and then assess your progress toward goal completion on a scale of one to ten.

WORKSHEET 1.10. Assessment of Recovery Goals

List your major recovery goals and then assess your progress toward goal completion on a scale of one to ten, where one represents little or no progress and ten shows a high level of progress.

Goal 1. _____

Progress Rating: 1   2   3   4   5   6   7   8   9   10

Goal 2. _____

Progress Rating: 1   2   3   4   5   6   7   8   9   10

Goal 3. _____

Progress Rating: 1   2   3   4   5   6   7   8   9   10

Goal 4. _____

Progress Rating: 1   2   3   4   5   6   7   8   9   10

Goal 5. _____

Progress Rating: 1   2   3   4   5   6   7   8   9   10

Goal 6. _____

Progress Rating: 1   2   3   4   5   6   7   8   9   10

Goal 7. _____

Progress Rating: 1   2   3   4   5   6   7   8   9   10

Goal 8. _____

Progress Rating: 1   2   3   4   5   6   7   8   9   10

Goal 9. _____

Progress Rating: 1   2   3   4   5   6   7   8   9   10

Goal 10. _____

Progress Rating: 1   2   3   4   5   6   7   8   9   10

CONCLUSION

It is a maxim in business that proper planning improves performance. The most important performance of your life is how you develop, implement, and work a recovery plan. This lesson has given you a blueprint for this process.

Lesson 2

Relapse Prevention and Recovery Maintenance

UNDERSTANDING RELAPSE

A Crash Course in Relapse

Addiction is a twenty-four-hour disease. Although it may now be in remission, it will be with you for the rest of your life. The disease can be activated at any time. We know from the definition of addiction that it is a disease process that is chronic and characterized by relapse. Similar to other diseases (e.g., cancer, arthritis, and migraine headaches), for addiction the reality is that relapse is quite possible—some would even say probable. This is a concern and worry that must be kept in mind. It is important to do all you can to prevent the activation of your illness and to manage it quickly and effectively if a lapse or relapse occurs. This is particularly true during the first year of recovery, when your mind and body are getting used to day-to-day living without the effect of chemicals in the nervous system, and you are learning new knowledge, skills, and behaviors designed to support recovery and lead to serenity.

Learning the skills and knowledge to stay sober is similar to learning any other skill. You must acquire the skills and practice them regularly. When you make a mistake, you must accept it and return to the strategies and approaches you have learned that are designed to strengthen and solidify the skill. For example, if you were learning to ice-skate, you would be spending a great deal of time getting used to

Managing Your Recovery from Addiction
© 2007 by The Haworth Press, Inc. All rights reserved.
doi:10.1300/5485_02

what it feels like to be on skates and keep your balance as you learn to propel yourself forward. Inevitably, you are going to fall over on the ice, but what do you do? Scream and yell and say, "What's the use?" and take your skates off and fling them? No! You pick yourself up and continue with the process. Falling down when learning how to ice-skate is part of the process, even a necessary part. Each time you make a mistake, you learn from the process and correct your behavior. This same approach and attitude can be applied to learning relapse-prevention skills and knowledge. If you make a mistake—that is, you pick up a drink or a drug—you accept it and recommit to a recovery program. You do not have to get judgmental or emotional about it. Yes, the costs of returning to alcohol or drug use are much greater than those involved in making mistakes in learning a skill such as ice-skating.

It is also true that becoming critical or judgmental with yourself, catastrophizing about your mistakes, and interpreting them as signs that you cannot stay sober is of little use to you. If you must go through these thoughts and feelings, go through them. Eventually, you must reinstitute a recovery program—and the sooner the better, for obvious reasons. Take mistakes in the learning process for recovery in your stride. You have made a strategic recovery plan. Work it! Return to it if you have a slip and again use a drink or a drug.

Research and clinical experience have shown that the chief causes for relapse behavior are either intrapersonal or interpersonal. Intrapersonal processes are internal experiences such as negative mood states (e.g., rage, anger, grief, depression, and anxiety) and negative changes in thinking, beliefs, and attitudes. Examples include asking yourself, "What is the use?" despairing, giving up, judging, criticizing, and telling yourself you are inadequate or a loser. These are problems with cognitive and affect management. During active drug addiction, you used alcohol or drugs for mood and affect management; for example, alcohol calmed you down, made you feel temporarily less depressed, or quelled your anger. It may have also affected your thinking process by temporarily giving you a new attitude toward a situation. (It is interesting that some bars advertise Happy Hour as "Attitude Readjustment Hour"!) During active addiction, you used substances to modify and manage moods and deal with uncomfortable feelings. In sobriety, you no longer have the impact of the same chemicals in your nervous system. This means that you have to develop other ways to manage distressing moods and affects (feelings). You must learn appropriate coping responses. You must learn to tolerate and not "awfulize" negative mood states or troubling emotions. You must learn to recognize dysfunctional thoughts and beliefs and not impulsively act upon them. You must learn to face uncomfortable situations rather than avoid them and to take advantage of the learning you can acquire from facing them. You should be on top of your moods, emotions, and feelings in recovery. If you are blindsided by them, you are vulnerable to a relapse. You should understand and anticipate your moods and feelings. You need to find out how you can cope with feelings in a natural way. If you do not learn these things, then a relapse to active addiction is almost assured.

The other chief cause of return to active addiction is related to interpersonal factors or social problems. Most interpersonal problems are directly or indirectly related to managing conflict. Conflict in interpersonal relationships is inevitable. Most chemically dependent persons react to conflict in one of two ways. They either overreact to it and become, for example, enraged, hysterical, and out of control, or they avoid or suppress it, swallowing it, ignoring it, and pretending that it is not there. Neither of these two extreme responses to conflict is very useful in maintaining recovery. Given that you have had, and will continue to have, conflict's with others in your life, including your spouse, your boss, co-workers, friends, and potentially anybody else walking or driving around the planet, you simply must develop adaptive ways to deal with conflict. There is no way around it. People do not have to act the way you think they should act. It is nice to have others, especially those with whom we are intimate, meet our psychological needs, but they are not bound to do so. People in your work environment are occasionally going to continue to act inappropriately. They will continue to vie with you for power, status, and influence in the workplace. Your children are going to be disrespectful to you. No matter how hard you work and what you attain, the people around you are not going to appreciate you as much as you think they should. Individuals you supervise and manage at work are going to continue to make mistakes and frustrate you. Your spouse or significant other may fall out of love with you. You may get fired. You may get tailgated tomorrow when you drive to work. All of these situations involve conflict. Managing conflict means that you have to take on an adaptive, useful orientation to it, including your thoughts, attitudes, and beliefs about others. Learning skills to maneuver through conflict situations with a minimum of emotional impact is crucial. Successful recovery demands that you understand yourself more and also that you understand others.

Both intrapersonal and interpersonal factors involved in relapse can generate what is known as a high-risk situation for you in recovery. The combination of a high-risk situation and the lack of an appropriate adaptive coping response, including the necessary skills and knowledge, can lead to a relapse to active addictive illness. For example, your spouse calls you and tells you that he or she does not love you anymore and wants a divorce. This is a high-risk situation. You are going to experience overwhelming feelings. You are going to be emotionally reactive. You may feel depressed. You are probably going to become judgmental and critical. If you do not have an appropriate coping response (e.g., calling someone in your support network or your sponsor, praying, meditating, taking a time-out, journaling your feelings), the chances of drinking or drug use are very high. Preventing relapse and staying sober, especially during the first year of recovery, essentially involves successfully maneuvering through high-risk relapse situations, which are chiefly tied to emotional or interpersonal problems for which we do not have an adequate coping response. By completing this section of your workbook, you will raise your awareness of high-risk situations for relapse and you will become more knowledgeable about, and skilled at, adaptive responses to high-risk situations.

Essential Knowledge About Relapse

Even after you gain some measure of stability and serenity in sobriety, the potential always remains that internal and external forces will reactivate the disease of chemical dependency. This can lead to the dismantling of a recovery program and a return to active alcohol or drug use in the form of a lapse or a relapse. A lapse is a slip defined as the initial use of a substance after an individual has made a commitment to abstain from maladaptive behaviors, feelings, and thoughts originally associated with active addiction.

Certain clear warning signs generally herald relapse, including the following:

- A noticeable increase in feeling stressed
- The emergence of other compulsive behaviors, such as perfectionism, work addiction, gambling, compulsive spending, and sex addiction or promiscuity
- The emergence of significant periods of moodiness during which you may feel lonely, misunderstood, depressed, and hurt
- A loss of interest in engaging in a structured recovery program, so your life becomes haphazard: you stop taking care of yourself, you lose interest in going to meetings, and subsequently you lose the day-to-day structure in your life
- Feelings of losing control of your day-to-day behavior and your internal psychological life: you start avoiding others and become defensive if they question you; you start feeling less competent and confident about your ability to stay sober; you notice an increase in feelings such as grief and anger; you hide your problems from others; behaviors you engaged in during your active addiction start to rear their heads again; you neglect your physical health
- You begin thinking about alcohol and drug use: you become dissatisfied with your life in recovery and you begin to feel that it is not working or it is not fulfilling; you start becoming more irritated; you start to romanticize your alcohol and drug use, remembering only the fun times you had (euphoric recall); you stop praying and meditating; you forget about your strategic recovery plan and become hopeless and give up

One or more of these warning signs may appear before you actually begin active drug and alcohol use again.

Stages of Recovery

Recovery is a developmental process, and you will go through various phases in your recovery:

- The honeymoon stage. This usually comes when you leave inpatient treatment. You are feeling confident and rested and have a sense of hope. You feel renewed. The initial danger associated with active addiction seems to have passed and you may have a tendency to simplify the complex problem of chemical dependency.

- The reality stage. In this phase, you begin to realize that all of your problems do not simply go away now that you are abstinent and in a recovery program. Although abstinence from drugs provides a sense of relief, the challenge of living with life's problems goes on. In fact, managing recovery may bring on new problems. This is why it is important to have a solid continuing care program and to engage in regular counseling and attendance at meetings. During the reality stage, you begin seriously to solve problems without the use of alcohol and drugs.

- The decision stage. Approximately six months after the start of abstinence, you may feel that you must make major life decisions involving your family, employment, money, etc. Anticipating making major decisions is accompanied by significant stress. The general advice is to avoid making major life decisions at this point, or at least to take them slowly and think them through thoroughly. It is important to maintain a balanced life during this potentially stressful period.

- The phase of independence. This occurs after approximately a year of abstinence. You may begin feeling very competent and confident. The danger is developing a sense of complacency. You are not out of the woods yet, although you may feel that you are. During this phase, it is important to stay engaged in a recovery program and to renew your commitment to enhancing and cultivating sobriety.

- Emotional recovery. This stage is said to occur after approximately eighteen months of sobriety. Psychological conflicts, issues with self-concept and self-esteem, deep spiritual issues, relationship difficulties, and other complex emotional concerns begin to surface. During this phase, it is very important to take good care of yourself, to engage in counseling and therapy, and to be particularly aware of balancing and managing your moods and feeling states.

There are other ways of viewing the developmental process of recovery. The important point is that it is a lifelong process that tends to unfold in a sequential, predictable fashion. It is important to deal with recovery proactively and to anticipate concerns and address them as they arise.

HIGH-RISK RELAPSE SITUATIONS

Dealing with High-Risk Relapse Situations

A highly useful activity is to determine your feelings of competency in dealing with potential high-risk relapse situations. Competency is defined as possessing the necessary knowledge, skills, and strategies with which to manage a high-risk relapse situation effectively without drinking or drug use. Competency also implies a sense of confidence that you know you can apply the necessary knowledge and skills to manage a high-risk relapse situation and you are able to predict your performance in dealing with it. In taking a proactive approach to high-risk relapse situations, it will be useful to complete the inventory in Worksheet 2.1. The results will give you a sense of your overall competency and confidence in dealing with various relapse situations. They will also identify areas of your life that need to be addressed to further develop your competency and thus prevent relapse and maintain recovery.

Once you have completed this inventory, review your scores and focus on those that fall into the low-to-moderate range. These are areas to explore for your continued growth in recovery. A low score indicates that you are extremely vulnerable because you do not have adequate knowledge, skills, and strategies to manage the situation effectively. If you have obtained a low score in a particular circumstance or experience, it is best to avoid those situations or experiences that lead up to it or are associated with it. If you cannot avoid such situations and experiences, then you need to seek professional help.

Moderate scores indicate that you have some level of competency but need to build and/or refine it. You can begin to focus on acquiring the necessary knowledge and skills to deal with these situations through attendance at Twelve Step meetings, reading recovery literature, talking with your sponsor, and other recovery activities. Obviously, situations in which you show a high level of confidence are not

WORKSHEET 2.1. Relapse Competency Questionnaire

Listed below are a number of situations, circumstances, and experiences that could trigger a return to active alcohol and drug use. Please go over each item and imagine yourself right now in each of these situations. Once you have done that, rate your perceived sense of competence in coping with this high-risk relapse situation without a return to alcohol and drug use. The scale on the right represents a subjective measure of your competence ranging from one (low competence) to ten (high competence). Remember, competency is defined as possessing the necessary knowledge, skills, and strategies to cope successfully with a particular relapse risk situation. Be as honest as possible in assessing your current status.

High-Risk Situation	Competency Rating
Mood and Feeling States	
For no reason at all, I become extremely sad and depressed.	1 2 3 4 5 6 7 8 9 10
I begin to feel extremely tense, anxious, and nervous and the feeling will not go away.	1 2 3 4 5 6 7 8 9 10
I become enraged with someone whom I feel betrayed me.	1 2 3 4 5 6 7 8 9 10
I get a strong feeling that I just wish others would leave me the hell alone.	1 2 3 4 5 6 7 8 9 10
I begin thinking about all the pain I caused others during my active addiction, and I get extremely dissatisfied with myself.	1 2 3 4 5 6 7 8 9 10
I get a feeling of extreme anger that I am an addict, and the feeling will not go away.	1 2 3 4 5 6 7 8 9 10
I become extremely jealous of others' accomplishments and my own lack of achievements.	1 2 3 4 5 6 7 8 9 10
I feel that no one loves me and that I am basically unlovable.	1 2 3 4 5 6 7 8 9 10

(continued)

I feel cranky and irritable because I just cannot get a good night's sleep anymore.

1 2 3 4 5 6 7 8 9 10

I start feeling high levels of physical pain.

1 2 3 4 5 6 7 8 9 10

Everything starts going wrong and I feel like giving up.

1 2 3 4 5 6 7 8 9 10

I feel alone and alienated from God.

1 2 3 4 5 6 7 8 9 10

I am dissatisfied with my body and I feel sexually unattractive.

1 2 3 4 5 6 7 8 9 10

My spouse tells me that he/she does not love me anymore and wants to leave me.

1 2 3 4 5 6 7 8 9 10

My children tell me they are ashamed and embarrassed by me.

1 2 3 4 5 6 7 8 9 10

Things are going so darned well; I have been happy for months, and what the hell . . . why not I have a drink?

1 2 3 4 5 6 7 8 9 10

I fall into deep depression that will not go away for weeks.

1 2 3 4 5 6 7 8 9 10

I have a sinking feeling of despair because I have lost a lot of money.

1 2 3 4 5 6 7 8 9 10

I am so stressed out. I worry all the time. I cannot sleep and I am so damned tired.

1 2 3 4 5 6 7 8 9 10

I feel confused and think, "What the hell am I going to do with my life?"

1 2 3 4 5 6 7 8 9 10

I get demoted at work to a boring, dead-end job that I hate.

1 2 3 4 5 6 7 8 9 10

(continued)

(continued)

Interpersonal Factors

I find myself constantly arguing with my spouse.

1 2 3 4 5 6 7 8 9 10

My boss and everyone else starts criticizing me at work

1 2 3 4 5 6 7 8 9 10

My friends tell me they are uncomfortable because I am an addict and they no longer want to socialize with me.

1 2 3 4 5 6 7 8 9 10

I lose the promotion at work to a guy who is a real jerk.

1 2 3 4 5 6 7 8 9 10

I found out that my best friend is sleeping with my wife/husband.

1 2 3 4 5 6 7 8 9 10

I lose my faith in God.

1 2 3 4 5 6 7 8 9 10

I lose my capacity to perform sexually with my partner.

1 2 3 4 5 6 7 8 9 10

There is constant fighting going on at my home.

1 2 3 4 5 6 7 8 9 10

I keep getting taken advantage of by my friends.

1 2 3 4 5 6 7 8 9 10

I get a job transfer to a new city and state and I do not know anybody there.

1 2 3 4 5 6 7 8 9 10

I am out with my close friends and they keep coaxing me into having a drink.

1 2 3 4 5 6 7 8 9 10

It is Christmas time and I am with my family. Everybody starts arguing and I cannot stand it.

1 2 3 4 5 6 7 8 9 10

I find out that my teenage son is a drug addict and is also dealing drugs.

1 2 3 4 5 6 7 8 9 10

I find out that my drunk-driving sentence includes spending the next six months in prison over the weekends.

1 2 3 4 5 6 7 8 9 10

(continued)

My job drastically changes and I find out I do not have the skills to do it any longer.	1 2 3 4 5 6 7 8 9 10
I am fired from my job.	1 2 3 4 5 6 7 8 9 10
My doctors tell me that I have a serious medical illness.	1 2 3 4 5 6 7 8 9 10
I find out that I have to care for my elderly parents.	1 2 3 4 5 6 7 8 9 10
My former drug dealer becomes my next-door neighbor.	1 2 3 4 5 6 7 8 9 10
I screw up really badly at my job and cost the company thousands of dollars.	1 2 3 4 5 6 7 8 9 10

---

problematic for you. You can face them easily and you feel confident dealing with them. As recovery progresses, you can take this inventory several times. Your competency range will increase as time goes on.

Your Personal High-Risk Relapse Situations

Obviously, the inventory in Worksheet 2.1 is not exhaustive in scope. Everybody's own situation is different. There may be, and probably are, high-risk situations for you that are not included in the questionnaire. In Worksheet 2.2, write down those situations, circumstances, or experiences that you will confront or are confronting in recovery and rate your level of competency.

DYSFUNCTIONAL BELIEFS IN RELAPSE

Deep within our psyches lie what cognitive psychologists call *schemas*, or silent beliefs/assumptions that affect the way we think, perceive, feel, and behave. Many of these core beliefs are about addiction, the use of alcohol and drugs, and relapse. They can have a dramatic effect on sustaining or reactivating addictive behavior. Some psychologists believe that dysfunctional core beliefs also play a role

WORKSHEET 2.2. Your Personal High-Risk Situations

List the circumstances, situations, or experiences that you are confronting or will confront in recovery. In the column on the right, rate your level of competency using the scale from one (low) to ten (high).

High-Risk Situation	Competency Rating
1.	1 2 3 4 5 6 7 8 9 10
2.	1 2 3 4 5 6 7 8 9 10
3.	1 2 3 4 5 6 7 8 9 10
4.	1 2 3 4 5 6 7 8 9 10
5.	1 2 3 4 5 6 7 8 9 10
6.	1 2 3 4 5 6 7 8 9 10
7.	1 2 3 4 5 6 7 8 9 10
8.	1 2 3 4 5 6 7 8 9 10
9.	1 2 3 4 5 6 7 8 9 10
10.	1 2 3 4 5 6 7 8 9 10

in the etiology of addictive disorders. During abstinence and sobriety, dysfunctional core beliefs about addiction can become activated and can lead to a relapse to active addiction. It is therefore important for us to understand dysfunctional beliefs and thoughts and how they can contribute to ongoing chemical dependency. It is also important to undermine these beliefs and substitute them with more rational, adaptive beliefs.

Addicts often harbor a number of general beliefs with regard to drug and alcohol use, for example:

- Drug and alcohol use will transform personal experiences in a positive way.
- Drug and alcohol use will enhance social and physical pleasure.
- Drug and alcohol use will increase sexual performance and satisfaction.
- Drug and alcohol use will increase power and self-confidence.
- Drug and alcohol use will increase social assertiveness and attractiveness.
- Drug and alcohol use will decrease tension and other negative emotions.

You may hold any one or a number of these beliefs. In the early days of your addiction, these beliefs may have been self-evident. Initially, alcohol and drug use may have led to positive experiences. You may have experienced social and physical pleasure. You may have even experienced greater sexual performance. Feelings of power, prestige, and status may have risen for you. Temporarily, at least, you may have been able to camouflage or dilute negative emotional states. However, as you have probably learned in the treatment process, these changes were all transient and apparent. Substance use seemed to give you all of these things. At one point in your addiction, you may have believed that alcohol and drugs were essential to maintain functioning.

Many addicted individuals are predisposed to alcohol and drug use by the following factors, among others:

- Hypersensitivity to unpleasant feelings, emotions, or moods
- Low natural motivation to control behavior in favor of instant satisfaction and gratification
- Poor skills in coping with problems

- Automatically giving in to impulses
- An inordinately high need for excitement, and a very poor tolerance for feelings of boredom and frustration
- Very little concern about the future or the consequences of one's behaviors

Both these psychological predispositions and dysfunctional core beliefs about substance use can haunt you in recovery. If they are not identified, addressed, and worked through, they may contribute to the process of relapse.

In order to help you better understand the core beliefs or silent assumptions you have about drug and alcohol use and addiction, take the inventory in Worksheet 2.3.

After you have completed the inventory, focus on the items that you agreed with. These are considered erroneous, dysfunctional core beliefs or silent assumptions that could cause trouble in your recovery. Ask yourself the following questions when addressing these beliefs:

- Where is the evidence for this belief?
- How do I know that it is true?
- Is there any evidence that it is not true?
- Are there other ways of thinking about this belief?
- What would be the disadvantages of adhering to this belief?
- What would happen if I changed this belief?
- What do I see is the relationship between this belief and my feelings, moods, and behavior?
- If a close friend of mine had this belief, what would I tell him or her?

Your answers to these questions may help you modify your erroneous beliefs. Completing this inventory may be an eye-opener for you. At the very least, you should give some serious thought to the beliefs that you agreed with. Discuss them with your sponsor or therapist. Be frank, open, and honest about your internal beliefs. There is no sense in pretending. Maintaining a healthy, skeptical, inquiring attitude about things is quite useful. Develop an action plan to deal with any of these dysfunctional beliefs that you identify as potentially problematic for you in recovery.

WORKSHEET 2.3. Chemical Use Beliefs Inventory

Listed below are some beliefs about alcohol and drug use and addiction. Please read each statement and then circle whether you agree or disagree with the statement.

Belief	Agree or Disagree	
1. Life is basically boring without alcohol or drug use.	**Agree**	**Disagree**
2. Using alcohol/drugs is one of the best ways to increase my creativity.	**Agree**	**Disagree**
3. I really cannot function in life without the use of substances.	**Agree**	**Disagree**
4. Deep down inside of me, I know that I am not ready to stop using drugs and alcohol.	**Agree**	**Disagree**
5. Without drugs and alcohol, I really cannot cope with the pain in my life.	**Agree**	**Disagree**
6. Cravings and urges to use drugs or alcohol cannot be controlled.	**Agree**	**Disagree**
7. The quality of my life will not get any better even if I am sober.	**Agree**	**Disagree**
8. Deep down inside, I do not think I really deserve to recover from addiction.	**Agree**	**Disagree**
9. Staying sober requires an inner strength that I simply do not have.	**Agree**	**Disagree**
10. I will never be able really to be socially comfortable without using alcohol or drugs.	**Agree**	**Disagree**
11. Despite everything I have learned about addiction as a brain disease, I secretly believe I can control it with willpower.	**Agree**	**Disagree**

(continued)

(continued)

12. I am going to feel deprived for the rest of my life if I do not use alcohol or drugs again. **Agree** **Disagree**

13. I am not complete without alcohol or drugs; they give me something that I inherently lack. **Agree** **Disagree**

14. I do not care what they say: addicts are pathetic, second-rate screwups. **Agree** **Disagree**

15. Since I have the genes for alcoholism, there is really little I can do to stay alcohol free. **Agree** **Disagree**

16. I just do not have the strength to go through life without using alcohol or drugs. **Agree** **Disagree**

17. I will never be happy in recovery. **Agree** **Disagree**

18. Deep in my heart, I believe that the Twelve Steps and addictions therapy are really a lot of crap, and I think there is a way to drink in a controlled fashion. **Agree** **Disagree**

19. Addicts are basically incomplete, unhappy people who will always return to alcohol and drug use, no matter what. **Agree** **Disagree**

20. The costs of addiction are worth the pleasure that I get from alcohol and drug use. **Agree** **Disagree**

DISADVANTAGES OF RETURNING TO ALCOHOL AND DRUG USE

After a few months of recovery, you may experience a sense of complacency. The pain of active addiction is starting to fade into the distance. You may begin to forget what you learned in inpatient treatment. The more oppositional, defiant, or challenging aspects of your personality may come to the fore. You may even decide that you will try drinking or drug use again and see what happens.

We urge you not to do this. In inpatient treatment, you probably learned a lot about the medical consequences of alcohol and drug use. It is important to review the neuropsychological consequences that may be influencing your decision.

The fact is that alcohol and some other drugs of abuse dissolve parts of the nervous system. Alcohol use, in particular, shrinks the brain. Now, as executives and professionals, you have a vital need for your brain and central nervous system. Your problem-solving abilities, creativity, adaptive capacities, and interpersonal and organizational skills all have their basis in your brain and nervous system. You do not want to compromise your nervous system any more than you have to, and any more than you have already. You simply cannot afford to risk brain damage from alcohol and drug use.

The following summary of the major neuropsychological, neurocognitive, and neurobehavioral research (Weinreib and O'Brien, 1993) on the effects of alcohol and drug use on the human nervous system is designed to decrease the attractiveness of alcohol and drug use:

- First, the longer you drink and the more you drink, the greater the brain damage. MRI (magentic resonance imaging) studies reveal a high incidence of brain atrophy in chronic alcoholics. Alcohol consumption predicts white matter volume loss in the sulci, which are the little bumps and curves you see on the exterior of the brain in a picture or a slide. Alcohol use also enlarges the ventricles, which are the spaces within the brain filled with cerebrospinal fluid. Chronic alcoholics show a selective shrinking of frontal and parietal lobe structures. Research shows that widespread cortical atrophy tends to be more prominent in chronic alcoholics than ventricular enlargement, although both are likely to occur. Cortical atrophy is associated with duration of drinking and increases with age.
- Deficiencies in glucose, sodium, calcium, phosphorus, and magnesium are common in chronic heavy drinkers. These deficiencies affect the mental status of the drinker. This means that your mood, thinking, and perception can be altered by the lack of these chemicals. Alcoholics often show low thiamine levels,

which have been associated with poor performance on intelligence and other neuropsychological tests. The neurotoxic effects of alcohol seem to be most prominent in the frontal lobes of the brain. Damage here leads to problems with organizing, problem solving, and self-control. Damage to the liver caused by alcoholism can also cause cognitive impairment.

- Chronic alcohol and drug use leads to impairment in abstract reasoning, and in visual and spatial cognitive skills. Abstract reasoning is necessary in high-level problem solving, particularly in scientific and mathematical pursuits. Chronic alcohol use also leads to impaired memory. Fifty to 70 percent of chronic heavy alcohol drinkers entering treatment show some form of clinically significant neuropsychological impairment. Some studies show that alcohol use reduces interior hippocampus volumes.

- The most consistent evidence of behavioral impairment among alcoholics has been found on psychological tests that require cognitive abilities, such as visual/spatial and visual/motor skills, abstract reasoning, new learning, attention, and certain forms of memory. Alcoholics generally retain much of their intellectual capacity; however, they have difficulty with new learning. Eye/hand speed and coordination are reduced by alcohol use. Generally, vocabulary and general knowledge remain unaffected.

- Alcoholics regularly show problems in the frontal lobe, as evidenced by neuroradial tests. This results in deficits in executive functioning. Executive functioning involves strategic planning, the use of feedback from the environment, working memory, goal selection, sequencing abilities, and flexibility of thinking. All of these are damaged and compromised by alcohol use.

- Brain imaging studies have confirmed that alcohol-related damage to the brain is partially, or sometimes fully, reversible.

- Cocaine produces cognitive damage, compromising visual/spatial skills and memory. Deficits in abstract reasoning have been found among cocaine addicts. Studies show that 50 percent of cocaine-dependent individuals demonstrate some cognitive impairment on neuropsychological screening tests. Chronic cocaine users have problems with maintaining attention, learning new material, verbal memory, and work productivity.

- Methamphetamine causes brain cell death. Studies show that long-term methamphetamine abusers have altered brain chemistry indicative of nerve cell loss or damage similar to that found in people suffering from strokes or Alzheimer's disease. Some methamphetamine abusers become severely disabled and develop uncontrollable tremors similar to those seen in Parkinson's disease.

- Heroin abusers develop many comorbid medical problems that can lead to kidney failure and heart valve infections. These, in turn, can lead to microembolisms in the brain that affect brain functioning and integrity. Thirty-seven to seventy-nine percent of opiate users have been found to have clinically significant cognitive problems such as learning disabilities and attention difficulties. Inhaling heroin can lead to comatose states and large brain lesions in users.

- Inhalant users show substantial risk for neurocognitive impairment. They show cerebellar degeneration, cortical atrophy, and impairment in motor control, intellect, and memory. IQ loss due to inhalant use is considerable, with as much as a twenty-five point drop over a period of several years.

So the next time you begin thinking about using alcohol or drugs, consider the effects on the brain. As a businessman or woman, or a doctor, dentist, or other professional, you rely on the integrity of your brain.

COPING WITH LAPSES AND RELAPSES

Coping with High-Risk Relapse Situations

Once you determine those situations, circumstances, states, and experiences that pose a high risk for relapse to active addiction, you need to develop an inventory of coping responses to deal with them should they arise. Coping responses are those strategies you utilize to get yourself through the high-risk situation without a return to active addiction. Avoid or minimize, if you can, those high-risk situations for which you show a low level of competence. For both low- and moderate-competency situations, it is important to have some type of coping response available to you.

The following are illustrative coping strategies to utilize when you encounter a relapse situation for which you are at risk:

- Increase your attendance at Twenty-Step meetings.
- Read "How It Works" in the Big Book.
- Call four or five AA/NA members for support and feedback.
- Sit down and do a brief meditation.
- Take a hot bath.
- Go for a brisk walk.
- Get a massage.
- Read your strategic recovery plan.
- Take a moment to pray.
- Call your sponsor.
- Go to the gym and engage in vigorous exercise.
- Journal your feelings.
- Take a ride in the country.
- Make a list of the positive and negative consequences of using alcohol or drugs.
- Call your therapist and arrange for an emergency meeting.

Coping with a Lapse

The role of coping strategies is to delay impulsive, irrational behavior such as picking up a drink or a drug. They are also designed to distract and to supplant a dysfunctional behavior with a more adaptive one. In high-risk situations, commit to twenty-four hours of sobriety. Tell yourself, if you must, that you can always drink or use a drug later. If you do experience a lapse, it is important to stop, look, and listen to what is happening. A lapse is obviously a warning sign that you are in danger. As soon as you can, remove yourself from the abusing situation. Keep calm. Your first reaction may be one of guilt, self-blame, or shock. It may be one of extreme enjoyment. Allow these feelings to come to you, to rise, to crest, and then eventually dissipate. Resist the urge to be judgmental with yourself. A slip does not have to turn into a full-blown relapse. A lapse does not mean that you are a failure. It can be an important component of the learning process in gaining recovery. Always renew your commitment to sobriety. Resist the urge to think, "What's the use? I've blown it already, I might as well keep using." Focus again on the immediate and long-term benefits you are getting from sobriety. During these situations, it is important to engage in as much self-nurturing as you can. Resist the urge to make something out of your lapse.

After things have settled down, ask yourself the following questions: What events led up to my slip? Were there any early-warning signals that preceded it? What were these signs? How can I head off problems in the future? If you are involved in counseling, make the lapse or potential relapse the focus of your counseling sessions.

If you do experience a lapse, or if you are experiencing uncomfortable, difficult-to-control urges and cravings to use drugs or alcohol, it is also important after the immediate danger has passed to take a step back and look at the bigger picture. Be particularly aware of how you are living your day-to-day life. Perhaps you are working too hard. You may not be taking good care of yourself. You may not be leaving adequate time for rest, spiritual practices, stress management techniques, exercise, and pleasurable activities. You may be pushing yourself too hard. You may be preoccupied with conflict and emotional problems in your intimate relationships. It is important to let go, as much as you can, of those experiences and circumstances that are pinning you down in life and restricting your sense of inner freedom. Now may be the time to go on a spiritual retreat. It may be the time to reenter or intensify therapy. It may be time to recommit and reestablish balance in your life.

If You Do Relapse

Relapse is a fact of life when it comes to addiction. If you do relapse, be gentle with yourself. Be kind with yourself, but be firm and do not despair. Put yourself in God's hands. He loves you and will guide you back to sobriety. If you relapse, you are not worthless, inadequate, or a failure. These are all judgments and interpretations. This is the time to muster all the love you can for yourself. Others around you, including those you love, may be exasperated with you. They may be angry with you. They will probably be deeply frightened. Remember that just as active addiction is only a drink away, sobriety is also readily available to you. There is an old Zen Buddhist saying that reads, "Success in life is falling down nine times and getting up ten times." Pick yourself up, dust yourself off, and rejoin the rest of us.

Lesson 3

Dealing with Conflict in Recovery

UNDERSTANDING CONFLICT

How we understand, deal with, process, and respond to conflict is a major factor to consider in ongoing recovery. During active addiction, you dealt with conflict in a dysfunctional way. The psychological consequences of conflict may have been muted and diluted by the presence of chemicals in your system. On the other hand, the process of addiction brought its own inevitable conflicts, particularly with loved ones and employers. Active addictions may have introduced high levels of conflict into your life and taxed your capacity to cope and hold up. It is common for chemically dependent individuals in recovery to become exquisitely sensitive to conflict once a recovery plan is initiated and carried out. During the first few months of recovery, you may feel emotionally raw and stress sensitive, and you may be showing some of the delayed symptoms of the post–acute withdrawal syndrome. As a result, managing conflict may be very uncomfortable for you. Therefore, it is important to develop useful and adaptive ways to understand conflict and manage it when it arises.

Conflict is a part of life. It increases in frequency and severity during times of change. The lack or absence of conflict is actually an ominous sign. Its absence indicates that the parties involved are defended against sources of conflict. This may be seen in some marital relationships when a couple in counseling state that they never argue. This is not a positive sign. Early on in life we develop a style of man-

Managing Your Recovery from Addiction
© 2007 by The Haworth Press, Inc. All rights reserved.
doi:10.1300/5485_03

53

aging conflict that often depends on how our family dealt with it. Many individuals deny and avoid conflict. On the other hand, the presence of overt conflict is really no guarantee that two parties are working together effectively. Conflict, if not handled adaptively, is potentially destructive. Handled well, it can be creative and can lead to greater problem-solving skills. The consequences of conflict really depend on how conflict is managed. It is very important for you to manage conflict well in your recovery.

Conflict can be healthy or unhealthy. With healthy conflict, the participants involved understand the causes and the usefulness of disagreement. They understand that no two individuals always have the same point of view. They work together to further mutual goals in the relationship. With healthy conflict, disagreements are about the issues at hand and not about the personalities of individuals involved in the conflict. With healthy conflict, useful management strategies lead to a positive outcome. Unhealthy conflict, on the other hand, is destructive. Individuals involved do not stick to accepted rational guidelines and rules for conflict management. Unhealthy conflict involves personal attacks, and individuals act out of their own selfish needs. Unhealthy conflict definitely hurts those involved. Unealthy conflict is marked by processes that escalate and aggravate the conflict, such as defensiveness, self-righteousness, failure to listen to the other person, threatening behavior, intentionally hurting another, and attacking another's character. Healthy conflict is characterized by strategies that de-escalate conflict, such as active listening, sensitivity to the other party's feelings, a focus on issues rather than personalities, gestures of goodwill during conflict, open expression of feelings, and a mutual focus on finding alternatives.

CONFLICT MANAGEMENT STRATEGIES

A number of approaches can promote healthy conflict management and lead to a mutually satisfying resolution. One major distinction in approaches is the orientation to conflict management. A major difference in orientation emerges between a problem-solving approach to conflict and a win-lose approach. In the problem-solving approach, conflict is defined as a shared problem to be solved. With the win-lose strategy, conflict is seen as a competitive situation where one party tries to triumph or get one over on the other. With the problem-solving strategy, the focus is on building progress toward common goals, seeking creative solutions and agreements that are mutually acceptable and satisfying. The win-lose strategy, on the other hand, involves a selfish pursuit of one's own goals and efforts to force the other party into submission to one's will. Problem solvers use open, honest, and accurate communication of needs, goals, positions, and proposals. Problem solvers show empathy toward and understanding of the other's position and frame of reference. They avoid threats to reduce defensiveness. Power is viewed as shared equally between the two parties. Win-losers, on the other hand, use power to dominate the other side. They use deceitful, inaccurate, and misleading communication of needs, goals, proposals, and positions. They make no efforts to empathize with or understanding the other's position. Hostility is openly, destructively expressed and can even involve threats to the other party. Problem solvers communicate flexibility and creativity. They are willing to change or abandon a position if doing so promotes conflict resolution. They emphasize cooperative behaviors and trustworthiness. Problem solvers actively explore both the similarities and the differences in positions. Win-losers, on the other hand, show a rigid, stubborn adherence to their position in an attempt to force the other side to give in. They behave unpredictably. They work to increase confusion and ambiguity. They may use deception and confusion to build their advantage. They exploit the other side. They emphasize only the differences in their positions and the superiority of their own position.

Obviously, the general problem-solving approach to conflict management is simply more useful in establishing and maintaining healthy recovery.

Conflict Resolution Styles

People have predictable, definable styles of managing conflict. Categories include the following:

- *Avoiders.* Avoiders show a tendency to allow themselves to be interrupted, subordinated, and stereotyped in conflict situations. They do not deal with conflict assertively. They tend to be ineffective listeners who come across as indecisive, and apologetic and engage in griping and backbiting behavior rather than deal with the conflict head on.

- *Aggressive Conflict Managers.* These people take the "bull in the china shop" approach to conflict management. Aggressives show a tendency to interrupt others, subordinate them, and stereotype them. They dispense with appropriate eye contact and often stare intensely at the other. They may come across as arrogant. They conceal information. They camouflage feelings. They dominate. They can be abusive, blaming, and sarcastic.
- *Problem Solvers.* Problem solvers have the most adaptive conflict management style. They state feelings, needs, and wants directly. They maintain appropriate eye contact. They develop and manifest an air of competency. They are able to engage in self-disclosure. They share their opinions and feelings. They are effective listeners. They show skill in dealing with other people.

Take a few moments to describe in Worksheet 3.1 your typical approach to dealing with conflict.

Managing Conflict

Most of us have never learned how to approach and manage conflict. If you have much over conflict in your life, it will be very useful for you to keep in mind some very simple, but effective, strategies to manage it. You do not have to spend your life bickering, arguing, name calling, screaming, attacking, challenging, and criticizing. You do not have to lose your temper and get out of control in parenting your children. You do not have to fight constantly with your spouse. Conflict management strategies can minimize such behaviors.

Some simple conflict management strategies can be utilized at any time:

- *Negotiating.* Many married couples scream and yell at one another, and many parents engage in heated arguments with their kids. They forget that negotiation is one of the best ways to deal with a conflict. Next time you are in an argument, cool things down and have a discussion about what you are willing to do and not do to resolve the problem.

- *Compromising.* Compromising takes negotiating one step further. At the outset, everybody in the conflict agrees to give up something. Compromising allows you to save face and allows everyone to get at least some part of what they originally wanted. All conflicts are resolved through compromise. We cannot have it all, all the time, on our own terms. This is a narcissistic, egocentric position.
- *Taking Turns.* This is a simple but elegant way to deal with situations where resources are limited. It involves one party delaying gratification. For example, if you have only one television at home, the parties involved flip a coin and take turns watching it.
- *Apologizing.* Again, this is a very simple but powerful strategy. Telling someone that you are sorry and acknowledging that you have hurt his or her feelings is a powerful response to conflict. Try it some time. Its effects are often miraculous.
- *Soliciting Intervention.* With this strategy, you call in a third party to referee the situation and provide an objective, rational voice. The third party will utilize negotiation and compromise in bringing about a solution to the conflict.
- *Postponement or Time-Out.* This is particularly useful when two hotheads are involved in a conflict. Agree on a predetermined amount of time (e.g., ten minutes) when you walk away from your adversary and allow your feelings to cool down. Utilizing a time-out can dramatically reduce the likelihood of aggressive acting-out behavior or saying something nasty that you will regret later.
- *Abandoning.* This means giving up and walking away. If the costs of engaging in continual arguing and conflict outweigh the benefits, it may be useful for you to simply abandon the argument and give into the other person. This also has the advantage of being a useful bargaining chip the next time a conflict arises. You can tell the person, "I gave in to you last time, now it is your turn!"

Fair-Fight Guidelines

We have often told couples in marriage and relationship counseling that it is important for them to learn how to fight fairly. Couples

WORKSHEET 3.1. Your Approach to Dealing with Conflict

In the space below, describe your typical approach to dealing with conflict. Include examples from family relationships and the work environment.

who are happy and stay together somehow learn to use fighting to resolve problems in their relationship. Fair fighting involves promoting fair behavior and avoiding unfair behavior. If you are going to have an argument with your spouse, for example, we suggest you make an appointment and set some time limits and the agenda to be discussed. Do not argue over the phone or in front of others. Tell the other person what you expect to get out of the fight.

Fair-fight behavior includes the following:

- Taking turns speaking one at a time
- Allowing for time-outs
- Observing and following the rules you agreed upon
- Actively listening to the other person
- Showing respect
- Admitting wrongs
- Being specific
- Being open minded

The following are examples of unfair behaviors, and you should avoid them:

- Dredging up issues from the past and opening old wounds
- Going off on irrelevant tangents
- Ignoring the other person
- Threatening and intimidating behavior
- Making accusations
- Engaging in annoying behavior, such as changing the subject, interrupting, scolding, yelling, teasing, lecturing, and name-calling
- Giving someone "the silent treatment".

When the fight is over, some level of resolution should be achieved, even if this means that the resolution is only to continue the unfinished fight at another time. If the other person has apologized to you, acknowledge it. Do not carry any grudges or bad feelings after the fight is over. If you can, agree to specific behavior changes to reduce future conflict.

DETERMINING YOUR PERSONAL CONFLICT RESOLUTION STYLE

Please take the inventory in Worksheet 3.2 to get an idea of your dominant or characteristic style of dealing with conflict. When you take the inventory, think of your behavior during conflict situations, such as at home arguing with your family or dealing with a conflict in the work environment. In completing the inventory, however, just think about what you usually do in any typical conflict situation.

The results will reveal your dominant, or characteristic, conflict resolution style. If your highest score is in the first section (questions 1-10), your dominant style is avoidance. You tend to shrink from conflict situations. You act unassertively and after the argument or conflict situation is over, you feel resentment and discontentment.

If your highest score was in questions 11-20, your characteristic conflict resolution style is that of a problem solver. You honestly and directly communicate your needs and wants. You do not see the conflict situation as a win-lose situation. You freely negotiate and compromise to come up with a mutually satisfying solution. You feel comfortable in conflict situations. You are clear and direct. You do not carry around a lot of psychological baggage after a conflict, and you do not personalize it.

If your highest score was in the last section (questions 21-30), you are an aggressive conflict manager. You define conflicts as a win-lose situation. You attempt to impose your will on the other party. Others may see you as ruthless and unfair. The results of your conflict resolution tend to be defiance and rebellion in the other party. You may get what you want in the short run, but you pay a high price for your victory.

Close or equivalent scores in these three categories reveal that you show a mixture or combination of styles with no particular style predominating.

The results from the questionnaire will give you some indication of your dominant or characteristic conflict management style. If your style is that of a problem solver, handling conflict is probably not difficult for you. If you tend to be an avoider or an aggressor, you are paying a psychological price for the way you handle conflict. Aggressors alienate those around them. People begin to avoid them.

WORKSHEET 3.2. Conflict Resolution Styles Questionnaire.

Read each statement below and then circle Yes or No according to your own conflict style.

When I am involved in a conflict or argument,	Yes or No
1. I usually keep my mouth shut and keep my feelings to myself.	**Yes** **No**
2. I try to get the conflict situation over with as soon as possible, even if it means I do not give my side of the argument.	**Yes** **No**
3. I rarely tell the other person exactly what I think.	**Yes** No
4. I hardly listen and I just keep thinking of ways to get out of the argument.	**Yes** **No**
5. I find myself apologizing, even if I did nothing wrong.	**Yes** **No**
6. I usually allow myself to be interrupted frequently.	**Yes** **No**
7. I never tell the person what is really going on inside of me.	**Yes** **No**
8. I usually feel a lot of resentment and anger in side, but I do not express it.	**Yes** **No**
9. I become very concerned about upsetting the other person.	**Yes** **No**
10. I tend to back off easily and placate the other person.	**Yes** **No**
11. I usually clearly state my feelings, needs, and wants to the other person.	**Yes** **No**
12. I maintain appropriate eye contact and communicate a sense of competency.	**Yes** **No**
13. I try to see and communicate the problem as something mutual to be solved. I do not take it personally.	**Yes** **No**

(continued)

(continued)

14. As much as possible, I try to understand the other person's position.	**Yes**	**No**
15. I do not hide or camouflage my internal feelings.	**Yes**	**No**
16. I avoid threats and ultimatums.	**Yes**	**No**
17. I look for useful, creative solutions to the problem.	**Yes**	**No**
18. As much as possible, I deliberately avoid hurting the other person's feelings.	**Yes**	**No**
19. I avoid domination or power plays.	**Yes**	**No**
20. I do not blindside the other person with surprises or dredge up past conflicts to put the other person in a "one-down" position.	**Yes**	**No**
21. As rapidly as possible, I try to dominate the argument and win it.	**Yes**	**No**
22. I interrupt, scream, yell, and do anything I can to win the argument.	**Yes**	**No**
23. I never let the other person know what I am actually feeling inside.	**Yes**	**No**
24. I have a tendency not to listen to the other person, but instead to plan what I am going to say next.	**Yes**	**No**
25. I use intimidation to get what I want.	**Yes**	**No**
26. I tend to be blaming, sarcastic, and loud.	**Yes**	**No**
27. I do whatever I can within reason to get my needs met.	**Yes**	**No**
28. I do all I can to assume a superior position.	**Yes**	**No**
29. I tend to be competitive rather than cooperative.	**Yes**	**No**
30. I do not like making concessions and compromises.	**Yes**	**No**

Scoring Directions: Add up the number of "yes" answers and write the score in the space to the right.

Your score: ———

They cut themselves off from potential sources of support and guidance. This type of conflict management style destroys intimate relationships. If you have an aggressive conflict management style, you should get help for it immediately. Avoiders tend to internalize the psychological effects of their conflict management style. Codependents tend to have this type of style. Avoiders hold feelings inside; they carry around grudges and deep feelings of resentment and discontent, but they rarely appropriately express them or engage in problem-solving behaviors designed to resolve them. Both avoidance and aggressive conflict styles may be appropriate in certain situations, but if they are characteristic of your behavior, then you should take a serious look at your conflict style and take steps to modify it.

UNDERSTANDING THE ROOTS
OF PROBLEMS WITH CONFLICT

The best way to understand any problems you have with dealing with conflict and getting past problems in this area is to focus on your beliefs about conflict. We all harbor beliefs known as silent assumptions about how life works. These beliefs are on the unconscious or preconscious level and we carry them into any conflict situation in which we become involved. The following are some examples of beliefs you may harbor that can make conflict situations difficult for you:

- I shouldn't have to deal with conflict.
- Others should just do as I say.
- Discussing problems is a waste of time.
- Arguing with someone is a sign that something is very wrong.
- If I avoid conflicts, maybe they will just go away.
- Arguments are a personal attack on me.
- People should just get along.
- I resent having to confront others.
- Conflict always hurts someone.
- Arguing with someone never solves problems.
- Nice guys finish last.
- Do unto others before they do unto you.

Silent assumptions or beliefs are embedded in our awareness. Usually we do not think about them or recognize them. Silent assumptions about conflict usually have their genesis in our experience in our own families. For example, if you grew up in a dysfunctional alcoholic family, you may have witnessed destructive, hurtful arguing. You may have walked away from that experience feeling that all arguing and all conflict are destructive and should be avoided. This is what many adult children of alcoholics and codependent individuals do. On the other hand, you may have felt so vulnerable and unprotected that you identified with the aggressor in your family and saw this as a way to acquire a sense of safety and stability as well as a way to get your needs met. You may have developed an aggressive conflict management style. You may have learned from your family that the best defense is a good offense. If you were fortunate enough to grow up in a fairly functional family, you probably learned that conflict was an inevitable and even necessary part of family life, that reasonable people could disagree, and that conflicts would lead to deeper intimacy and the solving of family problems. What we learn about life in our formative years, we can carry through our lifetime. As the psychoanalysts say, "The child is the father of the man (or woman)."

Take a few minutes to think about life growing up in your family. Look back and think about how your parents and brother and sisters handled conflict within the family. For example, picture your family around the dinner table or at another family gathering. How did your family argue? Did they engage in fair or unfair fighting, or a combination of both? Were you able to express your feelings, both negative and positive, openly and honestly? Was conflict destructive? Did it frighten you? Were family members made to feel bad if they openly and honestly expressed differences of opinion? Were your opinion and feelings solicited by other family members? Were they respected? What did you learn about handling conflict from your family-of-origin experience?

In Worksheet 3.3, write down your beliefs about dealing with conflict in your life based on your early experiences.

Now that you have reflected on and written down your beliefs, assumptions, and the lessons you learned about dealing with conflict based on your early family experience, it is time to do something

WORKSHEET 3.3. Your Beliefs About Dealing with Conflict.

In the space below, describe your beliefs about dealing with conflict based on your early life experiences.

about your beliefs. Maybe you are okay with them. Maybe you are uncomfortable with them. Maybe you just never thought about them before, and now that you have, you see that many of these beliefs are irrational or erroneous and should change. As you go over the beliefs that you have listed, ask yourself the following questions:

- Is there any real evidence that this belief is true? What am I basing it on?
- I there an alternative way to think or believe?
- If I do not change or modify this belief, what effect is it going to have on my life from here on?
- If someone else espoused this belief about conflict and told me about it, what would I think of it? What would I tell them?
- Did I choose this belief? Do I have to keep on believing it?

Identifying and challenging erroneous beliefs associated with your conflict management behavior is the most basic and powerful way to resolve difficulties you have with conflict resolution. When you realize, for example, that you are imposing unrealistic, irrational, useless, dysfunctional expectations on others, or on yourself, you begin to see your role in conflict difficulties. You begin to take responsibility for problems you have in managing conflict in your life. Eventually, you can see that these beliefs or assumptions are often arbitrary and do not have any evidence to back them up. Just because your beliefs or assumptions made sense when you were a child growing up in your family does not mean they have to make sense now and that you have to continue to adhere to them. Drop your dysfunctional beliefs and assumptions. As much as you can, enter into conflict situations with a non judgmental, innocent orientation. Take conflict as it comes. Play it as it rolls. Even enjoy it! After all, if it is an inevitable, unavoidable part of life, you might as well make it as pleasurable as possible.

Lesson 4

Managing Feelings and Moods

UNDERSTANDING FEELINGS AND MOODS

Our feelings or emotions are the lifeblood of our existence. Imagine a life without feelings, if you can. Think of Mr. Spock on the old *Star Trek* series. As a Vulcan, he had no feelings. All he had were intellect, logic, and reasoning. Despite his brilliant intellect, the character was a hapless fellow who evoked compassion. After all, what kind of existence is a life without feelings? If we did not have them, we would experience only thoughts and physical sensations. The feeling of love in all its forms and manifestations is perhaps the most important feeling in life, the one we pursue most, and the one that guides our day-to-day motives and actions. Can you imagine a life without love?

Yet feelings can be troublesome. We shrink from feelings of unhappiness, grief, sadness, guilt, anxiety, and despair. During active addiction, alcohol and other drugs were used to modify and change troublesome emotions and supplant them with at least temporary feelings of pleasure and happiness. However, as addiction progressed, the positive effects of the chemicals diminished. Positive feelings were nowhere to be found. Instead, they were eclipsed by horrible moods and feelings such as sadness, desperation, grief, and fear.

It is important for recovering persons to understand the phenomenon of feelings. Feelings are very much akin to physical sensations. Actually, feelings are an extension and differentiation of physical sensations, although they are much subtler than sensations such as

Managing Your Recovery from Addiction
© 2007 by The Haworth Press, Inc. All rights reserved.
doi:10.1300/5485_04

touch, taste, and sight. We need only look to common parlance to see that this is true. Consider the following expressions:

- I got really hot under the collar when he insulted me.
- I was touched by his show of affection.
- The tension in the room was so thick you could cut it with a knife.
- She is an emotionally cold person.
- My heart swelled with love for my mother.
- I got so mad, I saw red.
- I was so nervous I felt butterflies in my stomach.
- His mood is black.
- A heavy sadness descended upon her.

All of these expressions show that physical sensations and emotions are very much intertwined. However, physical sensations rarely cause us problems in life. If you were sitting in a room and somebody whacked you in the knee with a hammer and you cried out in pain, nobody would blame you. People would probably sympathize with you. However, if somebody insulted you and you lost your temper and screamed at them, you might be criticized by others as out of control, childish, moody, overly sensitive, and "a hothead."

You may feel the same feelings about yourself. For many, identifying and expressing feelings is very difficult. We may be uncomfortable with the expression of feelings in others and ourselves. Showing feelings involves a risk. Showing feelings runs the risk of hurting someone else's feelings. We can be judged or criticized by others if we honestly manifest our feelings. Our feelings can be used against us. To others, they may illuminate vulnerabilities that can be exploited.

Growing up, we may have learned powerful messages about experiencing and showing feelings. In some families, for example, the expression of both negative and positive feelings is strictly taboo. Other families are hyperemotional: feelings are never contained or regulated, and they come out all over the place. Most of us learn that some feelings are okay to express, but others are not. For example, it may be okay to express feelings of glee or happiness, but expressing feelings such as jealousy or dissatisfaction is not seen as appropriate.

We all develop very deep, often unyielding, beliefs about what is acceptable with regard to the experience of feelings and the expression of them. We tend to gravitate toward others who share our beliefs and ideas about feeling expression. We may avoid those who show a different emotional style than we do because it makes us uncomfortable and we do not understand it. Our beliefs about feelings can cause us a lot of trouble in life, as we shall soon see. For example, some of us believe that we should control our feelings at all costs. We suppress feelings. We are dishonest with others and ourselves about our feelings. Sometimes this makes us literally sick, and we begin to experience psychosomatic complaints, such as stomachaches and headaches. Others may view us as uptight. We go through life unaware of our emotional life.

It is important for recovering individuals to understand feelings. As the neurotoxic effects of alcohol and other drugs wear off in abstinence and recovery, feelings we have repressed and anesthetized for decades start to activate and resurface. We must learn how to recognize and manage our feelings and moods in recovery. We have to learn to deal with feelings. Psychologists call this skill *affect tolerance*. This refers to the ability to allow a feeling to express itself consciously without controlling it. We initially tolerate it and become used to it, and we see that the expression of feelings cannot hurt us. With affect tolerance, we adopt a non minding, innocent approach to feeling identification and expression.

If you have suffered a lengthy addiction, you may be totally ignorant of what and how you feel. The expression of feelings in recovery can be bewildering and frightening. We will now focus on understanding the nature of feelings and moods and managing troublesome negative feelings and moods.

In general, we are attracted to experiencing and amplifying positive emotional states and reducing or eliminating negative feeling states. As we will learn, feelings rarely come out of the blue. They are usually embedded in our thoughts and beliefs and arise during specific circumstances and in specific situations. Our feelings are mediated by our autonomic nervous system and our limbic system. The latter is the same system involved in pleasure and reward associated with drug and alcohol use. Feelings are also conditioned by stress. When you are stressed out, your body kicks into a state of high physiological arousal that makes you more apt to express feelings.

Feelings can be both simple and complex. Examples of simple feelings are sadness, grief, anger, and excitement. Simple feeling states can congeal and become integrated into more differentiated feeling states. The role of the thought process is more dominant in complex feeling states. Examples of more complex feelings are jealousy, contempt, wonder, and incompetence. Feeling states are not mutually exclusive. We can actually feel a composite of a number of feelings, both simple and complex, at any given time. For example, when you fall in love you may simultaneously experience a mixture of love, fear, ambivalence, wonder, awe, compassion, and apprehension. Interestingly, the experience and expression of feelings often evokes meta-feelings, which are feelings about feelings. For example, you may feel a strong physical and emotional attraction to your boss at work and subsequently develop a number of feelings such as fear, disgust with yourself, and disappointment. You begin to have strong feelings about your experience of a feeling that you see has undesirable repercussions.

From a psychological perspective, because feelings can be so uncomfortable and threatening, the ego develops defense mechanisms to manage them. Defense mechanisms give us a sense of self-control, they help us maintain self-esteem, and they help us control our behavior in response to feelings. Many defense mechanisms can be cited. Common ones include

- *Denial.* This is probably the most common and most virulent defense utilized by alcoholics and addicts. With denial, we lie to ourselves. Denial distorts reality. With denial, we massively ignore what is real. We refuse to accept reality. There are many forms of denial. *Minimizing* involves watering down or diminishing a feeling. *Rationalizing* is making excuses. For example, we are rationalizing when we state that we need to take pain-killers because we have lower back pain. *Intellectualizing* is another form of denial. We protect ourselves from uncomfortable feelings by ignoring them and retreating into our intellect. We stick to facts, ideas, and concepts rather than allow ourselves to experience a feeling state.
- *Attacking.* Attacking is another psychological defense. When we feel hurt, we strike out at others and put into practice the axiom that "the best defense is a good offense."

- *Protection.* With protection, we take an unacceptable feeling and attribute it to someone else. We utilize psychological defenses in an effort to maintain psychological balance in life. Psychological defenses are useful. However, if they are too strong or we utilize too many of them, we may block ourselves out of feeling much of anything in life. Part of psychological health is developing a healthy level and constellation of psychological defenses.

The ways we defend against uncomfortable feelings are not only psychological, they can also be chemical, as during addiction. When we drink or drug, we reduce or eliminate uncomfortable or unacceptable feelings and we amplify positive feelings, such as pleasure and euphoria. Chemicals are powerful defenses against feelings. The use of alcohol and other drugs to control feelings really works—for a while. Eventually, however, drugs lose their pleasure-inducing effects and the emotional debt we have built up by chemically suppressing negative feelings needs to be paid. In the later stages of addiction, for example, we may experience chemically altered, uncomfortable, negative feelings and moods. When we start out drinking or drugging, we are operating in the "normal" zone of feelings and emotions—that is, normal for us. When we use alcohol and drugs, our mood elevates and expands out of the normal range into the range of euphoria or intense pleasure. In the beginning, the greater the amount and frequency of alcohol or drug use, the greater the level of euphoria. When the drugs leave our system, we return to our normal, usual, characteristic zone of feelings.

However, as our addiction progresses, the swing to euphoria does not go as far. We need more and more of the substance and get less and less of an effect. At the same time, when the drug leaves our system, we are not returning to the same set point of normal feelings or moods for us. We are beginning to experience a drop in mood from normal feeling states to painful ones. At some point in our addiction, we start feeling "not quite right" after drugs and alcohol have left our system. Feelings of pain and discomfort begin to grow. After a while, we start to use alcohol and drugs to assuage this continual feeling of emotional pain. However, the more drugs we use, the less euphoria we experience, and eventually the pain-diminishing effects of alcohol and drugs wear off. In the later stages of addiction, the addict finds him or herself in a state of continual emotional pain. For a time, the use of alcohol and drugs may make the individual feel somewhat normal, but eventually even this sense of normality goes and horrible feelings such as constant tension, anxiety, despair, depression, and terror take its place and become the dominant feeling states.

We know that this process at the level of feelings has a physiological counterpart. The more alcohol and drugs we use, the greater our tolerance to the effects of drugs. At the same time, the neurotoxic effects of alcohol and drugs are beginning to have a degenerative effect on our nervous systems. Chronic alcohol and drug use can actually cause neuropsychological damage to the nervous system and affect our capacity to feel and think in a normal way. This is why continuous abstinence is so very important, especially during the first year of recovery. We have to give our nervous systems the chance to normalize and self-repair. We need proper nutrition, rest, and balance in our life as we heal. As the body heals, the mind will heal also. This healing process will bring into focus feelings, emotions, and moods we have suppressed or altered for many years. Troublesome feelings and moods will demand our attention. We may need formal psychotherapy, counseling, or medications to deal with severe mood problems such as depression, rage, and anxiety. However, even if we do not require these interventions, every chemically dependent individual has to learn to accommodate to and live with his or her feeling life. Old emotional wounds need to be acknowledged so they can be healed. Repressed feelings have to emerge. "Frozen feelings," or feelings we have held in abeyance, need to unfreeze, and we may need to experience an emotional meltdown. In recovery, we need to stop being afraid of feelings. Feelings are not facts. They simply exist just as any physical sensation does. Feelings are not right or wrong, appropriate or inappropriate. When we allow the emergence of the full range and continuum of our feelings, we start coming into the experience of our true self. We reclaim the totality of our personhood. We stop self-denying and experience the fullness of life. This is one of the wonderful gifts of recovery. We recover ourselves as feeling persons. We accept all of our feelings and allow their expression, even if only to ourselves. We let go of judging ourselves for having certain feelings.

Feelings Exercise

In Worksheet 4.1, describe yourself as a feeling person. First, list any beliefs or attitudes you may harbor that render the recognition, expression, and disclosing of feelings difficult for you. Next, write down those feeling states that you find particularly troublesome. To assist you with this, Exhibit 4.1 lists various feeling states. You can review this list and select from it those feeling states you find are problematic. When you write down the feelings, be particularly aware of those feeling states you attempted to dilute, cover up, or eliminate through active alcohol and drug use.

RECOGNIZING, EXPERIENCING, AND DISCLOSING FEELINGS

It may be helpful as you progress in recovery to rediscover and explore feeling states and moods you have neglected, abandoned, denied, ignored, or modified during your active addiction. As you learned in the lesson on relapse management, what we do not know will hurt us. What we do not know about our emotional functioning could blindside us and put us in a psychological state that makes us vulnerable to relapse to active addiction. It is therefore important to raise our level of emotional awareness and work to get past those psychological processes we use to inhibit the experiencing of feelings. We need to let go of needless emotional control. There are times when control of emotions and impulses is appropriate. It is not, however, healthy for us to walk around twenty-four hours a day in an emotionally controlled state. Finally, we need to become comfortable and skilled at sharing and disclosing our emotions, feelings, and moods. This can lead directly to greater intimacy, self-understanding, and empathy for the psychological struggles of others in our lives. Getting in touch with our feelings can raise our level of social and *emotional intelligence,* as psychologists call it. When we are in touch with our feelings, we can be better lovers, dads, moms, friends, bosses, and co-workers. On the job, we become better managers, supervisors, and salespersons because we intuitively understand others and ourselves much better. We can become more productive and

WORKSHEET 4.1. Describing Yourself As a Feeling Person

Describe yourself as a feeling person. First, list any beliefs or attitudes you may harbor that render the recognition, expression, and disclosing of feelings difficult for you. Next, write down those feeling states that you find particularly troublesome. Be particularly aware of those feeling states you attempted to dilute, cover up, or eliminate through active alcohol and drug use.

EXHIBIT 4.1. Feeling States

Inferior	Humiliated	Hopeful
Disappointed	Clumsy	Annoyed
Desperate	Inadequate	Delighted
Stopped	Let down	Fulfilled
Calm	Childish	Light
Ashamed	Unseen	Jumpy
Irritated	Poor me	Endless
Gloomy	Strong	Defeated
Unnoticed	Horrified	Rejected
Grieved	Used	Hopeless
Complete	Terrified	Despised
Lonely	Put down	Withdrawn
Pitiful	Guilty	Attracted
Washed out	Jealous	Needed
Disgusted	Compassionate	Stingy
Alone	Hurt	Close
Foolish	Serene	Unwanted
Weak	Heavy	Satisfied
Seen	Alarmed	Bold
Grateful	Confident	Cloudy
Shy	Frustrated	Sad
Giddy	Frantic	Spiritual
Loved	Content	Empty
Positive	Relieved	Unhappy
Unneeded	Secure	Refreshed
Crushed	Tough	Suspect
Brave	Unrewarded	Happy
Needy	Stepped on	Appreciated
Risky	Frightened	Helpless
Craving	Timid	Humble
Scared	Captivated	Powerful
Jittery	Cornered	Gutsy
Ridiculed	Quiet	

effective at our jobs and our family lives. When we are blind to our own emotions, we cannot understand others' emotions.

Recognizing Feeling States

One of the most rapid and effective ways to get in touch with the nature of a feeling is to focus on your body. To assist in raising your awareness of a feeling, sit back and relax for about five minutes. In your mind's eye, go over your body from the tip of your toes, up your legs, through your stomach, into your torso, down your arms, and up into your neck and head. Become aware of any sensations in your body, such as tightness, warmth, cold, rigidity, numbness, tension, or tremulousness. Next, allow your awareness to gently focus on that body part. The sensation could be in any part of your body, but those associated with emotions may cluster around your heart or your solar plexus, your chest, the small of the back, and the neck. Just allow your awareness to hover and penetrate the area of your body where you are picking up a physical sensation. Gently observe the feelings or emotions associated with or connected with these physical feelings and sensations.

Ask yourself the following:

- How would I describe this feeling to another person?
- What does this sensation remind me of?
- How intense is it?
- When I experience this sensation, what emotion does it evoke in me?
- What memories or associations do I have for it?
- What does this sensation feel like?

Once you get clear about the nature of the feeling, ask yourself the following questions:

- How do I feel about this emotion?
- Could I express it to someone else?
- Is there anything "wrong" with this feeling?
- What word can I use to describe the feeling?

Just innocently and effortlessly allow yourself to experience the feeling. Tell yourself that it is okay to experience the feeling. After a few minutes of sitting in relaxed silence, you can refer to the feeling list to help get a better verbal description for the feeling. Taking the time to practice this simple feeling exercise can significantly develop your skill at recognizing feeling states you may have ignored previously or were unaware of.

Disclosing Feelings

Once you have recognized and allowed yourself to experience a particular feeling state, it may be useful to express it. You can do this verbally by shouting, screaming, saying what is on your mind when you experience the feeling, taking a paper and pencil and drawing the feeling, or writing the feeling down. If someone is available, you can talk to a trusted friend and just allow your feelings to come out. Let go of any preconceived ideas about feeling expression. Do not edit or judge your feelings. If you feel deep sadness, say so. If you feel like crying, let it go. If you feel anger, let that surface. Avoid the tendency to make something out of the feeling state. After you have allowed the feeling to be expressed, you may want to write it down in your personal feelings journal. This could be particularly useful if you need to clarify the feeling and get a better understanding of it, which is important for feelings that you may want to communicate to loved ones, friends, and others in your life at a later time.

Dealing with Troublesome Feelings and Moods

Reclaiming our feeling life is an important developmental task in the first year of recovery. Sobriety is about experiencing ourselves as feeling persons. However, the experience of feelings and moods can also be troublesome. As we get sober, painful feeling states may come to dominate our emotional functioning. For example, we may feel out of control with anger or rage. We may struggle with feelings of deep sadness and depression. We may have anxious, worrisome feelings that distract us and keep us from focusing effectively in our professional and personal lives.

We may experience strong feelings of irritability and agitation with others. Good emotional health is experiencing our emotions in a balanced fashion. It is normal to have occasional days when we feel sad or blue, periods of nervousness, or periods of anger. However, when these feelings become so intense and frequent that we lose the quality of our lives, it is time to do something about them. In this section, we discuss ways to bring out-of-control feelings back into balance and into the normal range of emotional expression. How will we do this? It is very difficult directly to change or modify any feeling state. Try it some time. The next time you feel a deep sense of sadness or a flash of anger, try instantly changing it. It does not work. As mentioned previously, feelings are very much interconnected with physical sensations and are basically extensions of them. A temporary way to change a feeling state is relatively easy. For example, you can take a few minutes to relax, take a shower, take a walk, practice some deep breathing, or meditate. These methods can all help when a feeling (anger, for example) is out of control. However, to make a fundamental, sustained change in feeling states, we have to change our thinking and beliefs. Think about it. Every time you feel an emotion or experience a mood, some mental activity is going on in your mind in the form of thinking. When you feel a feeling, chances are you are thinking a thought. Thinking and feeling, or cognition and emoting, are very much interconnected processes.

A neurophysiologist looking at the human brain sees rich neural interconnections between the limbic system and the cerebrum. Nerve fibers project from both of these areas into one another. The limbic system, of course, is the system in the brain that subserves and mediates the experience of emotion and pleasure. The cerebrum is the thinking part of our brain, where we experience thoughts, beliefs, and concepts and engage in problem solving and reasoning. Thinking and feeling are thus inextricably bound together from psychological, neurophysiological, and neuroanatomical perspectives. When we feel a feeling, we are thinking a thought. Therefore, when we are experiencing an uncomfortable or troublesome feeling, we are thinking a dysfunctional thought. Think about the most recent time you got angry. Maybe somebody insulted you at work by criticizing you. If you examine this situation, you will notice that just as you experienced the emotional and physical sensations of anger (e.g., feeling the heat rise in your body, your heart pound, and your breathing become more rapid and shallow), you were talking to yourself internally. You may have thought, "Who the hell does he think he is? How dare he embarrass me in front of my co-workers! He's an insensitive bastard!" The feelings of anger and the "hot cognitions" or thoughts of anger in your mind went hand in hand.

Think about the most recent time you got anxious or nervous. Maybe you had to speak in front of a large group. When you got to the podium, you began feeling shaky, your breathing became rapid and shallow, you experienced a dry mouth, you felt a weakness in your knees and butterflies in your stomach, and you were also talking to yourself internally. You may have been thinking, "What if I stumble and make a mistake? I'll look like a jerk. If I panic, everybody will know it and I'll look foolish. I hate public speaking. Why did I agree to do this? I know I'm going to blow it." Again, feelings of anxiety and fear coincided with internal self-talk. Both occurred simultaneously. Moreover, dysfunctional, irrational thinking and self-talk intensify a negative feeling state such as anxiety or anger. The more you tell yourself horrible things, the more anxious you feel. The more anxious you feel, the more you tell yourself horrible things. This kind of vicious cycle can be quite distressing for patients who suffer from panic and anxiety attacks. The vicious cycle spins out of control and it can be quite debilitating.

The key to changing painful, troublesome feeling states is to change the associated thoughts that accompany the feeling states. We also need to identify and change how we interpret situations and events that evoke feelings. Psychologists have identified several ways in which individuals who have emotional problems systematically distort emotion-evoking situations. If we can identify, describe, and understand these dysfunctional ways of interpreting emotional situations, we are in a position to challenge them and change them.

There follow descriptions of the distorted, erroneous, illogical ways (known as cognitive distortions) we think about or interpret situations that cause us emotional pain.

Emotional Reasoning

Emotionally reactive individuals utilize this cognitive distortion frequently. With emotional reasoning, we essentially say to ourselves, "Because I feel it, it is true." For example, you may feel extremely hurt in an argument with your spouse. You may erroneously conclude that your spouse is a hurtful person and that you are a vulnerable, emotional individual doomed to a life of continual hurt. If you do not feel good about yourself in a situation, you may conclude that you are inadequate or flawed, simply because you feel that way. You overemphasize the reality of your feelings. Just because you feel it does not necessarily mean it is true. It is just your interpretation of the situation.

Jumping to Conclusions

This is a common cognitive distortion. An example would be looking at your face in the mirror, noticing a mole or blemish on your skin, and immediately telling yourself that you have malignant skin cancer. Naturally, you then feel terror-stricken and panicky. You take one piece of evidence and erroneously conclude that you know exactly what it means, when in fact you do not. You can also do this with other people. Say you plan to meet a colleague for lunch and she is late for the meeting. You may jump to conclusions and say to yourself that this person is disrespectful and does not care about your feelings. You exclude all the other possibilities and focus only on the one you arbitrarily arrived at. In this case, jumping to conclusions makes you angry and irritated.

Overgeneralizing

With this cognitive error, you take one bad experience and see it as one episode in a never-ending cycle of negativity. For example, you go out to play your first golf game and really screw up. You conclude erroneously that you will never be able to learn golf and that every time you try to play, you will screw up again. You generalize from one unfortunate incident in the present to all instances in the future. If you break up from a romantic relationship, you conclude, "I will never be able to love again." If you take on a project at work that fails, you conclude, "I am washed up with this company. I will never get a promotion." Obviously, you then feel depressed, sad, and awful.

Personalizing

With this error in thinking, you erroneously conclude that you are the sole or major cause of problems in your life. If you have an argument with your spouse, it is your fault. If a meeting goes badly at work, you screwed up. If revenues for the quarter at your job are down, you conclude that they would be up if only you worked harder. With personalization, it is all about you. You forget that problems almost always have multiple causes and that no one person is the sole cause of anything. If you get divorced, you figure, "If only I had been a better spouse, my marriage would have lasted." The problem is that you have no proof this is true. You arbitrarily conclude that you are the cause of problems in your life.

Catastrophizing

This is also called awfulizing. You tell yourself that feelings or situations you are involved in are horrible and you cannot stand them. You assume that the worst will happen in any situation. If you lose some money on the stock market, you erroneously conclude that you are bound to go broke. Maybe you will become a homeless person, begging in the streets. With catastrophizing, your mind races to horrible conclusions. Catastrophizing has elements of both jumping to conclusions and overgeneralizing. However, with catastrophizing, you do not just jump to a conclusion: you jump to the worst one imaginable and firmly believe it.

These are all ways we regularly, systematically, and predictably misinterpret emotionally arousing situations and circumstances that we are involved in. We then regularly, systematically, and predictably make ourselves miserable! When we utilize these cognitive distortions, we talk to ourselves and tell ourselves horrible things. These distorted thoughts amplify and accelerate negative feeling states until they become very uncomfortable, and often until they get out of control.

How do we get out of all of this? There is a simple, relatively easily learned and implemented process for changing troublesome feeling and mood states. It involves becoming more mindful and aware of what we tell ourselves when we are engaged in situations that are evoking strong feelings. The first thing we should do when we notice a feeling spinning out of control is to slow down, step back, and ask ourselves, "What is going on here?" The next step is to examine what we are telling ourselves (our internal self-talk) while we are feeling particular emotions such as anger, depression, or anxiety. The next thing we do is examine and challenge the distorted, dysfunctional thoughts we are telling ourselves. After we have challenged their validity, we attempt to supplant these thoughts with more rational, adaptive, useful ones. If we do this often enough, we will eventually change our style of thinking, perceiving, and interpreting emotionally laden events and we will bring our emotions, moods, and feelings back into balance.

Here is a personal illustration of this process. A few years ago, I (Dr. O'Connell) was working as a clinical supervisor for an outpatient drug and alcohol counseling agency. Part of my job involved regular weekly group supervision of a staff of ten therapists. I took my job as clinical supervisor very seriously and responsibly. However, I quickly found out that the staff did not share my zeal and enthusiasm for supervision. I would come to our supervision time at the appointed hour to find only two or three therapists present. When this happened for three weeks in a row, I hit the ceiling. I became enraged and I lost my temper. I really lost my cool. I was screaming and yelling, and I even kicked a chair over. I was feeling all the obvious physical and emotional experiences of anger. This is how I interpreted the situation: I thought to myself, "Who the hell are these people? I have twenty years of experience as a clinical psychologist. Do they think they know more than I do? They think they do not need supervision! They have no respect! They obviously fail to see the value in getting clinical direction on cases. They are a bunch of clinical morons! This job is a waste of time. I am so sick of this. I can never get anybody to do what I want them to do! If my boss tells me I have to do supervision again, I am going to tell him to go to hell."

I got extremely angry because of how I interpreted the situation, and I aggravated this anger and amplified it by telling myself all sort of negative things. When you read the internal self-talk I engaged in, you can see a number of the cognitive distortions I have discussed, including overgeneralizing, jumping to conclusions, and personalizing. It turns out that I was wrong about a number of factors that I had misinterpreted and misperceived. Actually, the therapists had great demands made upon them with regard to time. They could not spare the time for regular weekly clinical supervision. The agency was such a bureaucracy that most of their time was spent in purposeless paperwork. Another group of therapists felt extremely threatened by group supervision. They felt vulnerable that others on the staff would find out about their knowledge and skill deficits as therapists. Most had not had clinical supervision by a psychologist in other work arrangements. They feared exposure. They had difficulty and struggled with feelings of inadequacy and performance anxiety in front of their peers. They actually liked me and saw that I had a lot to offer but were a little intimidated by me. Obviously this counseling agency had systemic organizational problems. It was poorly managed. Problems with job design left little time for reflective work such as supervision. The counselors were not rewarded for clinical excellence or signs of professional growth. Rather than check all this out, I simply flew off the handle. I found myself building up greater and greater levels of anger as the weeks went on. In many ways, I suffered needlessly. I could have checked out the reasons for poor attendance at clinical supervision time, but I did not. I also simply took the thoughts I was thinking at face value and did not challenge them or look for other ways of interpreting and understanding this emotionally charged situation.

You need to learn a simple method of defusing uncomfortable emotions and mood states. Exhibit 4.2 provides an example of the method; Worksheet 4.2 is a blank chart for your use. If you like, you can actually go through the steps and write down your feelings, thoughts, and counterstatements. (It is not essential, however, that you do so.) The following summary list the steps in identifying, challenging, and balancing negative emotions.

1. When you find yourself getting uncomfortable, stop. Your first emotional reaction to a situation is almost always wrong. Step back. Slow down. Do not be so reactive.
2. Go immediately to an examination of your thinking. What are you saying to yourself while you are experiencing this emotion? What are your automatic thoughts or self-talk?

3. Decide which cognitive distortion you are practicing. Are you jumping to conclusions, showing emotional reasoning, overgeneralizing, personalizing, or catastrophizing?

4. Challenge your dysfunctional, irrational, erroneous thoughts. You can do this by asking yourself one or all of the following five questions:

   • Is there any evidence for this thought? What am I basing it on? How do I know it is true?

   • Is there an alternative explanation for what is going on here, or is my explanation the only one?

   • If I just stayed with this thought and did not change it, what effect would it have on my emotions and on this situation?

   • If someone else told me they were thinking this way, what would I tell them about it?

   • Is this thought or idea something I have chosen, or is it just arbitrary, automatic, a reflex? Do I have to keep on believing and adhering to this thought?

5. Now step back and let go of your distorted thinking. You will notice an immediate change in your emotional state. Once you have challenged and undermined your erroneous interpretation of the situation, you free yourself up. You begin to look at things more rationally.

6. Develop a rational counterstatement or reinterpretation. Once you have identified the distortions in your thinking you can come to another conclusion, on that is more adaptive, rational, and useful. In the personal example that I gave, I could have told myself, "The therapists' absence from this meeting could have a number of causes. They are not necessarily being disrespectful and inconsiderate. I should check out what is going on more closely before I get so angry."

You can save yourself a lot of heartache and emotional anguish by implementing this simple process of stepping back, examining your thoughts, challenging them, and supplanting them with more rational and adaptive ones to modify the troublesome or uncomfortable feeling state that you are experiencing. We like this process because it is simple and practical, and it works. Get into the habit of examining your self-talk and internal thinking when you are beginning to become

EXHIBIT 4.2. Sample Dysfunctional Thought Record

Situation/ Emotion	Automatic Thoughts (Self-Talk)	Cognitive Distortions	Rational Counterstatements
1. I drank last night. I feel deeply depressed, hopeless, and angry at myself.	1. What's the use?! I'll never stop drinking no matter how hard I try. I just can't get it. The next relapse will be the end for me …	1. Jumping to conclusions Over generalizing Personalizing Catastrophizing	1. Hold on. Just because I had a slip doesn't mean I'll never get sober. I have to see what's missing and learn the skills to stay clean. If I keep thinking this way, I'll just block my chances to get sober. Lots of people have a slip and get back on track. It's not the end of the world. I can do it.
2. My time for a raise came up, but I did not get one. I feel angry, inadequate, and insecure.	2. This is bullshit! I deserve that money. He's got it in for me. He hates addicts. I'll bet his dad was an alcoholic. This means my days are numbered at this company. Who am I kidding, I'm going nowhere fast. I could get the axe at any time. What the hell am I going to do? I guess I'm screwed.	2. Jumping to conclusions Catastrophizing	2. I have no real proof my boss dislikes me. There are other reasons I don't get more money. I haven't considered them. If I keep thinking this way I *will* screw up my job. I don't have to concern myself with this. I'll just do the best job I can do. Even if I do lose my job, I'm not helpless. I've got options.

85

WORKSHEET 4.2. Dysfunctional Thought Record

Situation/ Emotion	Automatic Thoughts (Self-Talk)	Cognitive Distortions	Rational Counterstatements
1.			
2.			
3.			
4.			

upset or to experience a troublesome emotion. The more you practice this approach, the easier it will get, and the more quickly you will realize the benefits.

EXAMINING AND MODIFYING MISTAKEN BELIEFS

Where does our distorted thinking come from? What does our tendency to misinterpret emotionally charged situations depend upon? We can trace distorted thinking and negative self-talk to what cognitive psychologists call schemas. Schemas are deep core beliefs and assumptions we have about other people, our lives, and ourselves. In our formative years we learn them from our parents, other family members, teachers, and peers. They are the basic building blocks of our view of life. They are unconscious and outside our awareness. They are self-evident in the sense that we take them for granted and we do not even know we have them until we begin to examine them when we get into emotional difficulties. If we had the misfortune to grow up in an alcoholic or abusive family situation, we probably developed a number of irrational, erroneous, dysfunctional schemas or core beliefs. For example, individuals growing up in alcoholic households often learn, "Don't talk, don't trust, don't feel." Another example is "Nothing I do is ever going to be good enough" or "I shouldn't expect happiness in life." Unfortunately, schemas or core beliefs are taken as absolute statements of truth about others, the world, and ourselves. They are self-evident to the person who harbors them. If we could see into your mind, we would discover that you have hundreds, maybe thousands, of core beliefs. These beliefs silently, guide your thinking, perceiving, and feeling life.

The following is a list of core beliefs that many individuals subscribe to:

- I should always be happy.
- If somebody confronts me, it means they are attacking me.
- It is horrible ever to be wrong or incorrect.
- I have to do something perfectly or I will not do it at all.
- People should do what I want them to.
- I should never have to be inconvenienced.

- Horrible things can, and will, happen to me.
- I cannot stand negative feelings.
- If people really knew me, they would dislike me.
- Never show your true feelings—ever!
- I have to be number one, or else.
- It is dangerous to lose emotional control.
- I must push myself to the limit.
- A quitter never wins and a winner never quits.
- A person should never take risks.
- I have to be on top of everything.
- Failure is worse than death.
- I have to prove myself in life.
- You are either for me or against me.
- Tough times do not last, but tough people do.
- Never let them see you sweat.
- Do not trust anyone over thirty.

When you go over the list, you may realize that you subscribe to one or more of these erroneous core beliefs.

You can identify, challenge, and correct mistaken core beliefs just as you can distort thinking or negative self-talk. For example, once you have identified a distorted core belief behind your distorted thinking and uncomfortable emotional reaction by questioning the belief, you can ask yourself, "Where is the evidence for this belief? How do I know that it is true? Do I know enough about the situation to adhere to this belief? Is this belief useful for me? Does it promote my own well-being, growth, and development? Did I choose this belief, or did I just blindly accept it as a part of my experiences growing up?"

It may be more difficult to identify dysfunctional core beliefs than it is to identify distorted thinking because beliefs are implicit rather than explicit and obvious. However, it is useful to identify them, particularly in dominant or recurring emotional problems in your life. For example, if you feel uncomfortable being intimate and loving in a romantic relationship and you find that you cannot sustain a romantic relationship for any appreciable length of time, you should start looking for a hidden core dysfunctional belief that is guiding your thoughts, feelings, and behavior. You may believe, for example, that intimacy is dangerous. Perhaps you believe that you will never get what you want in life. Perhaps you believe that you should be suspicious about deep emotions such as love. You may believe, "Relationships are trouble. I should avoid them at all costs." If you do not examine and challenge your dysfunctional core beliefs, then you really are at their mercy. The best context for identifying and challenging core beliefs is in the therapy relationship. When you are in therapy, you devote a set time each week for self-examination and you have the assistance of a therapist in probing your defenses and blind spots and in facing the beliefs and conclusions you have arrived at about yourself, others, and life in general.

It takes time, tenacity, and courage to get to the core of emotions. Through a combination of engaging in the exercises explained in this lesson, Twelve Step group attendance, and good therapy work you can expect to bring your moods and feelings into balance. You can then begin to enjoy your feeling life in recovery.

Lesson 5

Managing Spirituality

UNDERSTANDING SPIRITUALITY

It may seem odd to think of spirituality as something that you manage. We typically do not think of spiritual matters that way. Spirituality seems somehow otherworldly and beyond mere human attempts to shape and influence it. We view spirituality in recovery as a very practical business and believe it is absolutely essential to have a solid spiritual program if you are to remain sober. Developing and maintaining a spiritual program in recovery is a major obstacle for many chemically dependent people. Spirituality is often associated with inspiration, and attempts to put it into a structure may seem inappropriate. We may feel that spirituality can be experienced or cultivated only when the spirit moves us. However, spirituality in recovery need not be an ethereal, haphazard, or chance affair.

We need only look to the great spiritual traditions that have existed for thousands of years to see that this is true. If you visited a Cistercian monastery in Massachusetts you would find that the monks there have a very structured day. For example, they regularly rise at 3:00 a.m. and recite the Psalms. They have daily structured meditation and prayer sessions. They eat and work at appointed times and they practice the Grand Silence throughout the day. A definite, carefully structured sequence of activities and spiritual practices make up their day. They follow the monastic rule of St. Benedict, laid down hundreds of years ago. If you were to visit a Zen monastery in Kyoto, Japan, you would find a similar atmosphere. The monks would rise together at a given time and practice *zazen* (or sitting meditation) for

Managing Your Recovery from Addiction
© 2007 by The Haworth Press, Inc. All rights reserved.
doi:10.1300/5485_05

91

a set number of hours. This may be followed by vigorous activity, a set time for physical labor, meals, and time to study sacred scriptures and recite the Buddhist sutras. The monks have a time for *mondo,* a personal question-and-answer session between student and Zen master. If you visited a Carmelite convent in the United States, an ashram in India, or a mosque in Iran you would likewise find a well-managed, sequenced, systematic program of spiritual technologies, activities, and approaches designed to culture the nervous system to experience higher states of consciousness that are the hallmark of spiritual growth and development.

The same rigorous and practical approach to spirituality is reviewed in this lesson. It is important to do as much as you can to maximize the chances for spiritual experiences and spiritual awakening. This is best accomplished through a systematic daily program for unfolding spiritual development. This lesson gives you some knowledge, guidance, and direction in this most important of endeavors. You need to manage your spiritual life in the same way that you manage your work life, personal and family life, and other aspects of your recovery program.

The following are the assumptions we hold about spirituality. First, spirituality is an abstract concept. It becomes operationalized in spiritual practices. The major operations are meditation and prayer. Other spiritual practices include physical approaches such as Hatha Yoga, Tai Chi, and devotion or service to God and others. Prayer and meditation are spiritual technologies. Their regular and systematic practice gradually cultures the nervous system, purifying it, stabilizing it, and ripening it for the experience of spirituality in all its forms and manifestations. The effects of spiritual technologies on the nervous system are cumulative, permanent, and irreversible. Each time you meditate or pray, a subtle change in the nervous system indicates a greater and deeper level of growth and purification. The subsequent experience of praying or meditating builds on this advancement. This process has been likened to the gradual ripening of a grape on a vine or an apple in a tree. With proper sunlight, hydration, and protection from disease and predators, these fruits slowly ripen until one day they fall off or are ready to be picked. Prayer and meditation ripen our nervous system as we gradually grow closer and more intimate with God or a higher power until one day we feel this union is completely stabilized and the basis of all our other experiences in the mental, psychological, emotional, and physical domains of our lives.

Today, the chief source of alienation and suffering in life is the loss of the spiritual connection to a higher power. The state of spiritual awakening and liberation is our birthright as human beings. It is not an exalted or mystical state. It is in fact the most normal state of human functioning. It is a state of joy, bliss, and innocence that we see in young children. However, the stresses of life and the socialization process inevitably erode this natural state, camouflage it, or cover it over until we feel that God is inaccessible, out of reach, or, in many cases, unreal. If you practice prayer and meditation on a daily basis and maintain continual abstinence you can again reclaim this innocent, effortless, happy style of functioning. In Twelve Step terminology, it is called serenity.

The scientific community has researched spirituality. Although we cannot research something as ineffable as the experience of God, we can research the effects of spiritual practices on mental and physical health, social relationships, work, and lifestyle. We now have the technologies to see the neurophysiological and neuropsychological changes imparted by spiritual practices. A brief summary of several of the more than 1,000 studies on spirituality will be presented in this lesson to give you empirical data on the benefits of working a daily spiritual program.

If you are working a Twelve Step program it is important to realize that AA is first and foremost a spiritual program. Implied in the Twelve Steps is that the ultimate origin of human problems, including addiction, is spiritual in nature and that the suffering associated with addiction is ultimately healed through spiritual efforts. AA is not merely a social support group, a folk psychotherapy group, or an opportunity for healthy socializing in recovery. It provides a set of principles and approaches designed to impart a spiritual awakening so that an alcoholic individual can live a happy, productive life in sobriety. The founders of AA realized that the spiritual is the most subtle and powerful of all the levels and layers of life. The word "spirituality" comes from the Latin *spiritus,* which means "breath" or "breathing." The act of breathing keeps us alive and allows life to continue and flourish. Without breathing, our life rapidly deteriorates and eventually is snuffed out. Breathing is life itself. It is vitality. The spirit is the unseen, unmanifested power that infuses our bodies and minds. Our bodies are the vehicles for this primordial power. Our bodies are both the expression and manifestation of spirit and its conduit in the physical world. The spirit is omnipresent. It is ever existent and uncreated. It is now and always will be. The spirit is our true nature. It is the part of us that we refer to as divine. The business of spirituality and spiritual practices is awakening to and realizing the higher nature or divine power that is at our source. When this power is fully realized our lives are transformed. Our fears diminish. We experience a sense of unshakable well-being. Problems come and go, but our identity in the spirit remains unshaken.

Although you may not have previously thought about it this way, spirituality can be a lot of fun. This may seem odd or even irreverent. After all, is not the realm of the spiritual sacred, holy, and serious? Spirituality is all these things, but it can be enjoyed as well. Spirituality is sheer joy. As one spiritual master put it, "When I meditate I become intoxicated with God." If you read the lives of the Christian saints or descriptions of spirituality by mystics and practitioners from other major world religions you will read about feelings of intense joy and happiness. Christian saints such as St. Teresa of Avila, St. John of the Cross, and St. Gregory speak openly and freely about the bliss that they experience when they commune with God. The fact is that God is a good time! In fact God is the greatest time! The practice of meditation, in particular, can infuse the nervous system with a sense of beautiful, subtle bliss and godly well being. The closer one gets to God or a higher power, the more pure and intense this bliss. So pray and meditate for the fun of it, for the sheer joy of it. Pray and meditate to stay mentally and physically healthy. Pray and meditate to stay sober, to cope with the stresses and strains of life, the traumas, the problems, and the disappointments. Finally, pray and meditate to celebrate the joys of life. The more you pray and meditate, the happier your life will be. For a more developed look at spiritual development, see D.F. O'Connell (2003c).

THE TWELVE STEPS AND SPIRITUALITY

The Twelve Steps provide a blueprint for spiritual development in recovery. All twelve of the steps reorient our awareness and consciousness. They help us see and acknowledge that we have experienced a sense of impotence or lack of power in our life due to addiction. They remind us that addiction has robbed us of mastery over our life and that it is time to regain it. The steps show us that we cannot reclaim our power through ego control or the power of will. These functions are necessary, useful, and effective in other areas of our life but not in the area of spirituality. A life based on sheer willpower is one of strain and fear. Will and control are not the answers. If they were we would simply stop drinking or drugging. Life is much too complex and varied to respond only to ego control or willpower. The steps therefore ask us to change our attention and develop a spiritual orientation to life. With this orientation we can activate the higher power that infuses, underlies, and informs all areas of our lives and utilize it for freedom from the bondage of addiction.

The Twelve-Steps of AA

We:

1. Admitted we were powerless over alcohol, that our lives had become unmanageable
2. Came to believe that a power greater than ourselves could restore us to sanity
3. Made a decision to turn our will and our lives over to the care of God as we understood Him
4. Made a searching and fearless moral inventory of ourselves
5. Admitted to God, to ourselves, and to another human being the exact nature of our wrongs
6. Were entirely ready to have God remove all these defects of character
7. Humbly asked Him to remove our shortcomings
8. Made a list of all the persons we had harmed, and became willing to make amends to them all
9. Made direct amends to such people wherever possible, except when to do so would injure them or others
10. Continued to take personal stock and, when we were wrong, promptly admitted it

11. Sought through prayer and meditation to improve our conscious contact with God as we understood Him, praying only for knowledge of his will for us and the power to carry that out
12. Having had a spiritual experience (awakening) as a result of these steps, tried to carry this message to alcoholics and to practice these principles in all our affairs

In step one it is implied that life is holistic, not just a bunch of parts and processes moving in all directions or random series of events and experiences. True living is not just getting by or hanging on by our thumbs but evolving and prospering. In this step we see how alcohol has fragmented our lives. This step also implies that God or a higher power has given us everything we need to master our lives and that we can tap into this power, which has lain dormant within us, camouflaged and distorted by the effects of addiction. Step one helps us retrieve our original nature. It shows us that what we have become is not what we truly are.

In step two we realize that our innate higher power is greater than our sense of powerlessness and impotence. We realize its capacity to penetrate our lives and restore us to our true nature. We realize that we are children of God. We have to wake up to accept our legacy, although at this point it may seem remote or even impossible. We are called to a higher purpose in life, that is, awakening to the spirit.

In step three we make the decision to rejoin God. We align ourselves with the God of our understanding. We let go of powerlessness. We hitch our carts to God and we set off in an entirely new direction, outward and upward.

In step four we take action. It is a step of undoing. We let go of obstacles that block our realization of our divine nature. We make a serious, penetrating examination of our current life orientation, which is one of bondage brought on by addiction. We see through and beyond this bondage to the reality of life. We begin intuitively to know that we can have a life beyond addiction, a life of freedom. Through our introspection and contemplation we begin to sort things out. We take on a new true direction.

With step five we acknowledge that our current state of affairs is untenable. We need to purge ourselves of all that is not God. We realize that we have either unconsiously or consiously worked at sustaining our addictive and compulsive behaviors. We acknowledge this not only to God and ourselves but also to another human being, which helps concretize and validate the process.

In step six we realize a profound truth in life: we cannot and do not have to do our own self-cleansing and remove our distortions and defects. That power that is the source of all of life will automatically do it for us. What we need to do is get out of our own way and let this innate inner power emerge. Our ego or willpower cannot cleanse us. With this step we tear down the walls of the dam and allow the purifying flowing water to wash over us and cleanse us.

With step seven we implement our acquiescence to the effortless, automatic purification brought on by our higher power. Through this, our sense of self expands beyond the boundaries we have erected.

In steps eight, nine, and ten, we complement the more passive process outlined in steps six and seven with active behaviors. We make purposeful, conscious efforts to allow healing to happen to others and ourselves. Similar to the prodigal son coming home, we rejoin our family and community. These steps are an antidote to the alienation and separation addicts and alcoholics experience. Through these steps we experience for ourselves our higher power operating in our lives, and we witness how it works. With these steps we realize that we are better than we thought we were. We can be honest. We can be humble. We can be compassionate and forgiving. We can be whatever the situation demands when our higher power is active and manifest in our life.

In step eleven specific instructions are given for advancement on the spiritual path. Here the spiritual technologies of meditation and prayer are introduced. Prayer is an active process of seeking union with our divine nature. Meditation, on the other hand, is generally considered a more passive process. The two work in a complementary, synergistic fashion. As mentioned previously, meditation and prayer are technologies that cleanse and stabilize the nervous system, allowing us to experience our divinity. They are techniques for transformation. Technique is involved in nearly all our activities from the simple and mundane to the highly complex. For example, a technique is involved in tying your shoes or your tie. Getting your hair cut involves technique. Painting your house, plumbing, carpentry, golf, swimming, and ophthalmic surgery all involve technique. In the same way, spiritual liberation involves technique. The techniques here are the various types of prayer and meditation. In step eleven we are exhorted to learn them and practice them.

The steps come to a conclusion with step twelve. With this step we open our arms to the rest of humanity. We take others in and we share our newfound freedom. We are no longer separate from others. We are back! Our hearts are stirred and compassion flows out of us. We become transformed. From here on in we take the position of giving in life rather than just taking or receiving, and with this newfound orientation our spiritual evolution expands exponentially with every life we touch.

The Twelve Steps culminate in a profound shift known as the *spiritual awakening:* a profound transformation, a new orientation toward life. Life will never be the same again following a spiritual awakening. The experience of spiritual awakening is a highly personal, intimate affair. It is often indescribable but self-evident to the one who experiences it. The spiritual awakening, however, is also a universal experience. The scriptures of the major world religions and spiritual systems all provide detailed descriptions of it. The experience of a spiritual awakening will come in as many different forms as there are individuals in recovery. It can come in small doses or it can be a dramatic, sudden, even shattering experience. It may even transpire outside of your awareness. One day you may realize that you have changed dramatically, that you feel quite different but you cannot pinpoint when your new style of functioning started. Often we are the last ones to know when we have experienced a change and only the feedback from others in our life gives some indication of it.

To illustrate the experience of spiritual awakening let me give you an account of the spiritual awakening of a patient. Her name is Jane. She is thirty-four years old, divorced, and was addicted to crack cocaine and alcohol. She was raised Roman Catholic but confessed that she never really felt much when she went to church. However, as part of her recovery she would drag herself to mass. One day she wandered into a chapel and sat in the back pew in silence. She recounts the following:

> I was sitting in the chapel and suddenly I had this intense realization that I could feel God's love in the room. I felt God's love to be real, to be swirling around the room entering my heart, mind, my feelings, and me. I felt as if I was in God's arms and I was being held to his chest. I began weeping. I felt God's

presence. I saw that we are all part of and parcel of God. And although I felt that God was separate from me, I knew that he wasn't. I was his and he was mine. I suddenly saw that there was another life for me beyond addiction. This affords one a life of sweet love, a life of service, and a life of connection with others. I had had this feeling in bits and pieces at other times during mass and AA meetings. But this time it was like a tidal wave washing over me. For the first time in my life I knew I was going to be okay. I had something that nobody could take from me. I felt so happy. I couldn't explain this feeling later when I tried to talk to others about it. I couldn't put it into words. But I know now that God definitely exists and he loves me and I can never be out of his love.

Another account comes from Steve. He is fifty-five years old, married, alcoholic, and the vice-president of a major manufacturing company. At the time of his spiritual experience he had been attending AA meetings three days a week for about six months. He was experiencing occasional urges to drink, but they were not particularly strong and he could cope with them. On one occasion he was sitting in a Twelve Step meeting on a weeknight and he had this experience:

I remember suddenly having the feeling that I didn't have to control things any longer. I was listening to members of the group tell their story and I began thinking of my own story. I remember my inpatient experience. I remember attending lectures on acceptance and surrender and how difficult it was for me to put aside the idea of willpower and ego. I consider myself a powerful man but I was humbled by my lack of control over alcohol. At this particular meeting I suddenly realized that I no longer had to play the control game. I realized that control was not something for me to exercise. That control, if in fact it even exists, comes from far beyond me. Far beyond any of us. I had a feeling of letting go. A kind of release. I felt relieved. I didn't have to control my drinking anymore. Something far beyond will handle that for me. I was never a religious person but suddenly realized that I was in contact with God, a power of such immensity that I felt a sense of awe. I realized that power had been here all along but I just was overlooking it. Maybe I was afraid to contact it. Maybe I was afraid that if I accepted this power that would somehow diminish me, make me feel smaller, less powerful. But all of that is gone now. I don't struggle anymore. I feel I rest in higher power. Life has become much more effortless. I enjoy my life now. I embrace my AA meetings. I truly feel that alcoholism was a gift. For I have something now that I never had when I was drinking. And I probably never would have gotten it unless I developed a drinking problem.

These testimonials give you some idea of the spiritual awakening. Every individual story is unique. However, the spiritual awakening is indeed real—perhaps the most real of all experiences. Talk to anybody who has had one.

SCIENTIFIC RESEARCH
ON SPIRITUALITY AND MEDITATION

More than 1,000 scientific studies have been published on the effects of spirituality on physical and mental functioning. These studies show appreciable, often dramatic, effects of spiritual practices on health. Consider the following:

- One hundred percent of studies over the past thirty years on addictions rehabilitation have shown the positive effects of spiritual and religious commitment on healing, health, and well-being in recovery.
- Survival rates for coronary disease are 50 percent greater for individuals with a strong spiritual commitment and practice than for individuals who have no spiritual program.
- Spiritually committed older adults show a 50 percent reduction in mortality rate compared with elderly patients without a spiritual commitment.
- Psychiatric patients who show a strong spiritual involvement record significantly lower anxiety, depression, and suicide attempts than patients who report no such involvement.
- A Blue Cross of Iowa study revealed that individuals practicing a type of meditation known as transcendental meditation showed a decrease of 87 percent for hospital admissions and a 50 percent decrease for doctor's office visits over a five-year period. Amazingly, these decreases increased with age, with the greatest benefits for those aged forty years and older. This is a direct reversal of the normal trend. That is, as we get older, we tend to get more medical problems and to use doctors and health care facilities more frequently.

Scientific Studies on Meditation

More than 650 studies have been conducted into meditation, specifically the practice of transcendental meditation (TM). During meditation, physiological and psychological impurities are gently removed. Research has shown that the practice of meditation gives rest that is twice as deep as that gained during sleep. Some meditation states such as Zen meditation, are associated with a heightened level of awareness. In devotional meditation practices such as Christian centering prayer, the meditator may experience an outpouring of bliss and love associated with the experience of union with God. Insight-oriented meditations impart a heightened sense of intuition and knowledge of one's own nature. Often meditations are so dramatic and profound that the meditator experiences a shift in the sense of self and is never the same again. From a psychological perspective, the practice of meditation can result in the dissolving of deep, firmly rooted stresses, that may be the source of a patient's fears, conflicts, phobias, anxieties, and mood disturbances. In our practice with recovering alcoholics and addicts, meditating patients regularly report dramatic decreases in cravings and urges to use drugs and significant decreases in compulsive behaviors such as gambling, sex, food, and work addiction.

The Physiological Effects of Meditation

Meditation and prayer can have profound effects on physiology and neurophysiology. Scientists have found that during the practice of a meditation such at TM the mind settles down to quieter and quieter levels of awareness and eventually "transcends" or goes beyond thoughts, feelings, and bodily sensations. The regular practice of meditation leads to the establishment and eventual stabilization of an integrated psychophysiological state known as *restful awareness* or *pure consciousness*. This state of restful awareness has been designated as a fourth major state of consciousness that is physiologically and biochemically distinguished from other states of consciousness: sleeping, waking, and dreaming.

During meditation the mind and body achieve a deep state of calm indicated by such parameters as a decrease in respiration rate and oxygen consumption, natural prolonged suspensions of breathing, a marked increase in skin resistance, and a decrease in arterial lactate and plasma cortisol levels. EEG (electroencephalograph) studies show increases in alpha- and theta-wave activity in the frontal parts of the brain and an overall increase in EEG coherence, both within the brain's two hemispheres and between them.

Figure 5.1 shows that the practice of TM produces a much more profound rest than resting with eyes closed, as indicated by increased

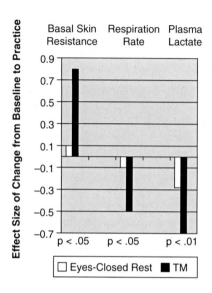

FIGURE 5.1. Physiology of Deep Rest: Physiological Changes During TM. (*Source:* Based on Data from Dillbeck and Orme-Johnson, 1987.)

basal skin resistance during TM, a lowering of tension, decreased respiration rate, and lower plasma lactate levels. All these suggest profound relaxation. High lactate levels have been associated with high anxiety and high blood pressure. These physiological changes occur spontaneously as the awareness settles down to its least excited state, known as *transcendental consciousness.*

Figure 5.2, shows that lower cortisol levels are achieved during the practice of TM, and these indicate a deeper state of rest than ordinary relaxation. Cortisol is a hormone that is elevated during stress. The study from which Figure 5.2 is taken shows that individuals practicing TM for three to five years have significantly lower cortisol levels during the TM technique than before beginning it and compared with a control group of individuals resting with their eyes closed.

Meditation and prayer have a dramatic effect on brain activity. The EEG is an extremely useful, noninvasive technique for evaluating cortical activity in the brain. In medicine it is used to indicate physiological disorders of the brain. Wires applied to a person's scalp at standard locations pick up low-amplitude electrical potentials from

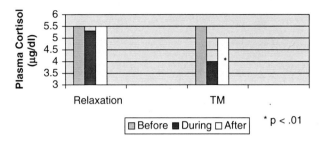

FIGURE 5.2. Biochemistry of Restful Alertness. (*Sources:* Jeving, Wilson, and Davidson, 1978; Evan, Symons, Beng, and Wellby, 1979.)

the cerebral cortex, the outermost part of the brain, which is responsible for thinking, feeling, and all higher-level cognitive functions. The EEG's voltage-sensitive needle registers any changes in the brain's electrical potential. Several patterns of brain activity can be described, and their presence is associated with various states of consciousness and types of thinking and emotional activity within the brain. Electrical potentials with a frequency of eight to twelve cycles per second are known as alpha waves. The presence of alpha waves indicates that the subject is alert and focused. Beta waves show a frequency of fourteen to thirty cycles per second. Their presence indicates tension and anxiety. Electrical potentials with a frequency of four to seven cycles per second indicate the presence of theta waves, which predominate before the onset of sleep. Delta waves are electrical potentials with a frequency of one-and-a-half to two cycles per second and their presence indicates deep sleep.

In Figures 5.3 and 5.4 we see the dramatic impact of meditation and prayer on EEG activity. Utilizing dynamic brain mapping, we can graphically view EEG changes after the onset of meditation and prayer. In the charts alpha waves are blue, beta waves are green, theta waves are pink, and delta waves are purple.

Figures 5.3 shows the EEG patterns of a subject (a) before, (b) during, and (c) after the practice of TM. During meditation alpha activity predominates, which indicates a state of restful alertness during which the meditator is tranquil, calm, but alert and aware. Figures 5.4 shows the EEG changes in a subject practicing repetitive Christian prayer (the rosary). In Figure 5.4b, during prayer, theta-wave activity predominates, indicating a deeply relaxed state.

Although not indicated by these single-subject research results, the effects of meditation and prayer are cumulative, and eventually one can permanently achieve a relaxed, coherent, serene, balanced, happy state of mind during all states of consciousness (sleep, dreaming, and wakefulness). This achievement is tantamount to a spiritual awakening.

The Effects of Meditation and Prayer on Addiction

According to the American Society of Addiction Medicine (ASAM) and the American Medical Association, addiction is a medical disease of the brain. Addiction is considered a biopsychosocial illness. Biological vulnerability, genetic predisposition, and environmental stressors combine to set the stage for the disease of addiction.

We have learned a great deal about how the brain works over the past decade, particularly the changes in function and structure of the brain after repeated exposure to drugs of abuse. Addiction, according to ASAM, disrupts the physiological mechanisms that are responsible for and underlie the generation, modulation, and control of our thoughts, feelings, emotions, and behaviors. Specifically, drugs of abuse activate the mesolimbic dopamine system of the brain, which is responsible for the mediation of reward and appetitive drives such as eating, drinking, and sex. The constant bombardment of the mesolimbic dopamine system by repeated drug use causes specific qualitative changes in the brain's functioning. For example, repeated alcohol use may enhance or reduce nerve cell response to everyday stimuli. Such neuroadaptation is said to lead to the development of tolerance and dependence, whereby higher and higher levels of alcohol are needed produce a psychoactive effect. Scientific evidence now shows that alcohol changes the brain's nerve cell communication by directly influencing the function of specific genes. Current research efforts are focused on precisely mapping the genes involved in alcoholism and other addictions. These research data will provide a greater understanding of the mechanisms involved in such experiences as dependence, tolerance, withdrawal, and cravings and of the mechanisms that cause or contribute to active addiction.

According to ASAM, the experience of stress plays a vital, although incompletely understood, role in the development and contin-

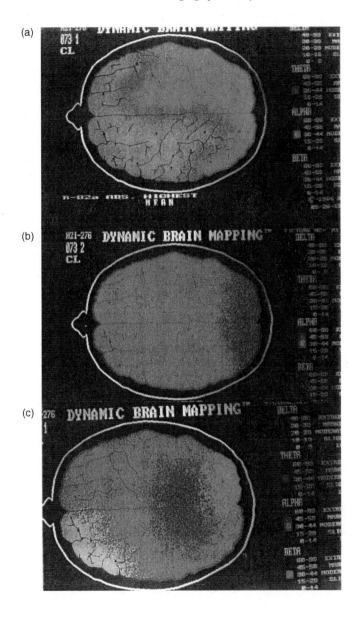

FIGURE 5.3. Changes in EEG During Meditation: (a) Prior to Beginning Meditation Practice; (b) After Five Minutes of Meditation; (c) Following Completion of Meditation. (*Source:* D.F. O'Connell, 2003b.)

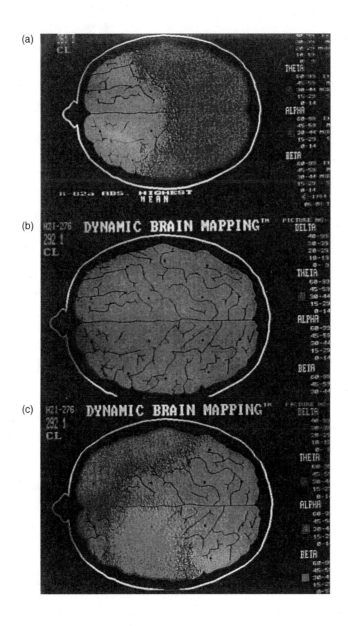

FIGURE 5.4. Changes in EEG During Prayer: (a) Prior to Practice of Repetitive Prayer; (b) After Fifteen Minutes of Prayer; (c) Following Completion of Prayer. (*Source:* D.F. O'Connell, 2003b.)

uance of addictive diseases. Experimental research has shown that various types of stressors increase the likelihood that an individual will self-administer drugs of abuse. Stress induces glucocorticoid (stress hormone) secretion, which in turn enhances drug-induced release of dopamine in the area of the brain known as the nucleus accumbens. The nucleus accumbens is considered one of the principle substrates of drug-reinforcing effects. Research has shown that a high intensity of stress and unpredictable stress have much greater effects on drug self-administration. High stress seems to raise the level of drug use because it modifies, at the neurobiological level, the motivation to take drugs as well as the reinforcing effects of the drugs themselves. Stress increases dopamine release in the brain. The use of drugs and alcohol can be a futile attempt by the stressed individual to regain normal psychophysiological functioning and balance. Drugs, however, provide only temporary relief and lead to even further dysfunction and imbalance. An individual's ability to maintain balance and cope with stress may be determined by genetics. Owing to genetic differences and defects, one or more of the mechanisms involved in the maintenance of internal balance, or homeostasis, may be impaired in certain individuals, leading them to abuse alcohol and drugs.

Chronic stress increases the body's production of cortisol. When cortisol is available at high levels in the body for prolonged periods, it can have many damaging effects. One of these effects is to induce the liver to produce enzymes that break down amino acids, which are the basis of neurotransmitters such as serotonin and dopamine. This decreased serotonin and dopamine availability leads to an inability to adapt to and deal with stress. When a decrease in serotonin availability due to chronic stress occurs, increased feelings of anxiety, anger, fear, frustration, and violence arise and can directly lead to the use of drugs of abuse. In addition, the subsequent use of alcohol and drugs causes further depletion of serotonin and continued physiological imbalance and emotional pain.

Breaking the Addiction and Stress Cycle

It has been shown that spiritual practices such as meditation can reduce or eliminate active addiction. Research indicates that the neurochemical changes resulting from the practice of TM may prevent or reverse the altered functioning seen in stress. These changes are cumulative and long term. The practice of TM also results in a decrease in cortisol, which leads to a reduction in physiological damage from this stress hormone. These effects are the direct opposite of the effects of stress and drug addiction on the brain and body. The increase in serotonin and reduction in cortisol brought about directly by TM indicate greater psychophysiological balance. The practice of TM reduces the chronic stimulation of the mesolimbic brain center (the anger and fear centers) and disinhibits the reward centers of the brain, thus producing profound feelings of well-being. These effects, over the course of time, become permanently established. This profound well-being in turn is associated with a decreased or absent desire for alcohol or other drugs of abuse. The practice of meditation can therefore interrupt the vicious cycle of drug use and replace it with a more virtuous cycle of ever-increasing balance and integration (O'Connell and Alexander, 1996).

EXPERIENCING MEDITATION

Meditation expands the experience of self. Regular meditation results in the establishment and experience of an unwavering, stable feeling of happiness that does not change with circumstances in life or even internal experiences such as thoughts, feelings, ideas, and sensations. The profound change in identity, that is the ultimate outcome of meditation has been termed *self-realization*.

Take some experiences of meditation reported by recovering individuals:

"During meditation I seem to drop away slowly. Thoughts become more distant and they fade away. I forget myself, yet I am awake inside myself. I seem to be 'me' without all the noises and chatter in my head. I feel what seems to be the source of love in my life. I accept everything in me and around me."

"When I meditate I really let go and let God, as the saying goes. I love not being in charge anymore. I love not paying attention to and worrying about details. It's as if I let the universe run the show for a while. I cannot imagine not having this experience in my life now."

"Recovery has been difficult for me. I constantly think of using. I miss using drugs. I am often bored and restless. When I meditate all of that goes away for a while. I forget any urges to use drugs. It's as if I am another person. When

I come out of meditation I feel renewed, more hopeful, and less overwhelmed with the demands of recovery. I seem to be less affected by all the stress and chaos around me."

Simple Meditation Practice

A simple, easily practiced technique is meditation with the breath. Breathing has been described as a spiritual lighthouse to guide us back to the present moment. We take breathing for granted. It goes on constantly in the background, and most of the time we barely notice it. Becoming gently and innocently aware of our breathing can be an effective way to induce a state of quiescence in the mind and physiological balance, thus purifying the body and mind of deeply rooted stresses.

Here are some instructions on meditation with the breath:

1. Find a comfortable posture, seated in a comfortable chair.
2. Close your eyes and gently and innocently become aware of your breathing. Just allow your attention to be with it for a few minutes.
3. Continue this awareness and allow yourself to settle into awareness of your breath. Allow your breath to just be. To come and go. To inhale and exhale. You may notice subtle variations in your breathing. Sometimes it is deep, as with a sigh; other times it seems to be rapid, coming in short bursts. Other times it seems to settle down, becoming more fluid. Your breath has its own inherent wisdom. It knows what it is doing. It simply and innocently breathes. It settles into its own rhythm and pace with each exhalation and inhalation.
4. Now become aware of various subtle changes in your breathing. Notice the slight pause between exhalation and inhalation. Allow your attention to settle on this brief pause or still point. Then allow your attention to focus again on the rhythm of your breathing. Breathing is very similar to the sea, flowing toward the shore and endlessly flowing back on itself.
5. Feel the air going in and out of your lungs; feel it coming in through your nostrils, filling you bronchial tubes and then your lungs. Simply notice the coming and going of your breath in your body. Allow a sense of peaceful awareness to settle on your breathing. Gently notice how your chest rises and falls with each

breath. Simply watch your breath. When thoughts, feelings, or physical sensations appear, simply note them and let them go. Return to your awareness of the breathing process. Just be with the endless tide of your breathing, in and out. Gently and peacefully.

6. Continue with this process for fifteen to twenty minutes. Then allow your awareness to settle into the present moment. After a few minutes gently open your eyes and resume activity.

Many forms and variations of breathing meditation exist, and two books are recommended: Victor Davich, *The Best Guide to Meditation* (1998); Joan Budilovsky and Eve Adamson, *The Complete Idiot's Guide to Meditation* (2003). Both books give step-by-step instructions on various types of meditation, including breathing meditation.

For optimum benefit, meditation should be practiced regularly, preferably after you rise in the morning and before supper in the evening for fifteen to twenty minutes. Regular meditation is a good stress management program. You should always approach meditation innocently and effortlessly. Do not be concerned with experiences during meditation. Resist the temptation to analyze any mental or emotional experiences you have during meditation. The practice of meditation produces profound purification and stress release. However, at times this process may become uncomfortable. Do not become overly concerned with any discomfort you may feel. When past stresses or painful memories come into your mind during meditation, just let them go.

Meditation is best learned from a skilled teacher. A number of meditation centers are located throughout the country where you can find a skilled teacher. Sometimes meditation sessions are followed by question-and-answer sessions designed to promote ease of practice and effectiveness of meditation. If one is serious about pursuing meditation it is important to find a reputable teacher or organization.

OVERCOMING OBSTACLES TO SPIRITUAL DEVELOPMENT

Any number of obstacles can block our efforts to devise and implement plans for spiritual development. Many of these obstacles come from experiences with religion and spirituality in the past. Our worldview and our view of the human condition may influence our spiritual development. For example, we may have a difficult time believing in God because of all the pain and suffering in the world. What kind of God, after all, would let this happen? Or we may feel unworthy of God's love because of things we did during our addiction. Many of our blocks to spiritual development are mental and come in the form of irrational beliefs, assumptions, and attitudes that become firmly entrenched despite the lack of evidence for them.

The following are some examples of thoughts, feelings, and beliefs that could block our spiritual development in recovery:

- I feel uncomfortable and hypocritical asking God or a higher power for things.
- I have never felt the presence of God, so what is the point of prayer and meditation?
- So much suffering goes on in the world, so how could there be a loving god to pray to?
- I was taught in my religion that God punishes us for our wrong-doings and I do not want anything to do with such a god.
- The idea of a higher power is such a vague notion. It really makes no sense to me.
- When I pray or meditate nothing happens. What is the point?
- My life is too busy to spend time praying and meditating every day.
- If God exists, he or she takes care of me and everybody else, so why bother to ask for his or her love and help? It is there already.
- I have to have a concrete sign that God is there before I can let go and place my welfare in his or her hands.
- Almost every religious person I know is a hypocrite. I see very little positive that can come out of spiritual practices.
- I have done so many bad things and hurt so many people during my active addiction that no god would forgive me.
- Addiction is a medical disease. How can a spiritual program fix something that is a physical problem? I need medical and psychological help, not prayer and meditation.

- If God cares for me and loves me, why did He or She let me become an addict and hurt so many people?
- Prayer and meditation are boring.

In Worksheet 5.1, list your own thoughts, ideas, and beliefs that may be blocking your interest in pursuing a spiritual program in recovery.

Once you have listed your personal views on spirituality in recovery, it is important to see whether they have any validity. You do this by challenging them and looking for evidence to support their validity. Ask yourself the following questions:

- Can I find any evidence that this thought or belief is true? What am I basing it on?
- Does any other, alternative explanation fit the thought or belief?
- If I do not change this thought or belief, what effect will it have on my life?
- If someone else had this thought or belief and told me about it, what would I tell them?
- Did I choose this idea or belief? Do I have to keep on believing it?

It is highly unlikely that you will develop, implement, and sustain a spiritual program in recovery if there are major obstacles blocking your spiritual pursuits. To help you overcome these obstacles, you replace the thoughts, beliefs, or ideas that block you from pursuing a program for spiritual development with more rational, adaptive ones. Exhibit 5.1 is an example. In the first column of Worksheet 5.2 list the blocking thoughts or beliefs that stops you from pursuing the recovery program. Ask yourself the five questions and write your responses in the middle column. Finally, in the third column substitute your blocking thought or belief with a more rational one.

After you have completed this exercise you will be more aware of how your beliefs influence your obstacles to establishing a spiritual focus in your recovery. By challenging your beliefs you may experience a greater sense of freedom and greater ease in designing a spiritual program for yourself in recovery.

WORKSHEET 5.1. Thoughts, Ideas, and Beliefs Blocking Spirituality in Recovery

List the thoughts, ideas, and beliefs that may be blocking your interest in and pursuing a spiritual program in recovery.

1.

2.

3.

4.

5.

6.

7.

8.

9.

10.

EXHIBIT 5.1. Sample Blocks to Spiritual Development

Blocking Thought or Belief	Challenging Thoughts and Beliefs	Rational Counter-statements
Belief 1		
Addiction is a medical disease and spirituality is not going to help heal it.	How do I know for sure this is true? Solid evidence suggests that addictive diseases can be healed through meditation, prayer, and other spiritual practices. Just because addiction is a medical disease does not mean it cannot have a spiritual component. After all, it has affected my relationship with God.	Addiction is a medical disease and spiritual practices may help in healing it.
		Spirituality can calm my mind and heal my brain and body.
	Very little advantage comes from hanging onto this thought. If I do I will not get any benefits from meditation, prayer, and other spiritual practices and I could rob myself of feeling better.	
	Nobody has come up with any proof that spiritual practices do not help medical diseases, so I cannot be sure about this.	
Belief 2		
God could never forgive me or love me again for all the horrible things I did to others during my addiction.	How do I know what God thinks? How can I presume to talk for God? I do not have any evidence this is true.	God created me and loves me and I can be open to His love and forgiveness.
	For all I know, God may love me and forgive me despite all I have done.	I am made in the image of God, who is all-loving and forgiving.
	If I hang onto this belief then I will never feel forgiven and I will be miserable. I will probably stay sick and use again.	

(continued)

What is the point of judging myself so harshly? Other people who have done worse things can get love and forgiveness from God, why not me?

Belief 3

I never felt anything when I prayed and meditated. Seems like a waste of time.	Do I know for sure that nothing positive happened? Research shows physical and psychological benefits to praying and meditating. Maybe I am just not aware of them.	Prayer and meditation are useful practices that can help me with spirituality and recovery.
	If I hang onto this belief I will not get the benefits of praying and meditating. There seems to be no advantage to believing it.	One does not have to feel anything special to benefit from meditation and prayer.
	Maybe I should not be looking for results in prayer and meditation.	
	How do I know that I will not eventually get benefits if I continue praying or meditating?	

Source: See D.F. O'Connell (2003b).

The following suggestions may assist you in developing an effective spiritual program:

- Identify and combat obstacles that block spiritual development. You should develop a plan to get beyond them.
- Identify, investigate, and integrate information on spiritual development from spiritual literature, audiotapes, videotapes, and a relationship with a spiritual mentor.
- Learn specific meditation and prayer techniques and practice them on a daily basis, preferably at the same time each day.

- Reconnect with your religious affiliation or faith by attending religious services regularly and reading the spiritual literature of your faith.
- Take a regular moral inventory (e.g., every two months) as directed by the Twelve Steps.
- Take care of your body with balanced nutrition, regular exercise, proper rest, and balanced work activities and relationships.
- Reconnect with nature on a daily basis; take regular walks and visit some natural areas such as parks, beaches, meadows, and gardens.
- Practice devotion by cultivating a sense of unconditional love and acceptance of others; selflessly give to them and engage regularly in the practice of forgiveness.
- Schedule regular spiritual retreats for extended periods of prayer and meditation at least twice yearly to deepen your practice of meditation in your prayer life.
- Reframing your addictive disease as a gift and spiritual wake-up call to a deeper, more meaningful life can provide an opportunity for unprecedented personal spiritual growth (See D. F. O. Connell, 2003).

A Daily Spiritually Oriented Schedule

Nature moves in rhythms and cycles. It cultivates spiritually. Practice of spirituality aligns your body and mind to the cycles of nature. The body loves a fixed schedule or routine. Following a regular routine is traditional in various spiritual heritages. Developing and maintaining a daily spiritual routine will maximize your spiritual growth and development. The schedule shown in Exhibit 5.2 would be considered an ideal spiritually oriented schedule for recovering individuals. By necessity it has to remain general, but it can be viewed as a general guideline for daily living.

It is best to rise daily between 6 and 7 a.m. This is the time when the world is waking up, and so is your physiology. Sleeping too late makes you sluggish, and getting up too early may leave you sleep deprived. Notice the mid-morning meditation and prayer break. If you take a coffee break, substitute it or augment it with a meditation break. If possible your midday meal should be your main meal and should be taken in a relaxed atmosphere. Follow it with a brief silence

WORKSHEET 5.2. Blocks to Spiritual Development

In the first column list the blocking thought or belief that stops you from pursuing your recovery program. Ask yourself the following five questions and write your responses in the middle column.

1. Can I find any evidence that this thought or belief is true? What am I basing it on?
2. Does any other, alternative explanation fit the thought or belief?
3. If I do not change this thought or belief, what effect will it have on my life?
4. If someone else had this thought or belief and told me about it, what would I tell them?
5. Did I choose this idea or belief? Do I have to keep on believing it?

Finally, in the third column substitute your blocking thought or belief with a more rational one.

Blocking Thoughts and Beliefs	Challenging Thoughts and Beliefs	Rational Counterstatements
1.	1.	1.
2.	2.	2.
3.	3.	3.

EXHIBIT 5.2. A Spiritual Schedule

Time of Day	Activity
6:00-7:00 a.m.	Rise, personal hygiene, and meditation practice
7:00-10:00 a.m.	Work/school
10:00-10:15 a.m.	Meditation/prayer break
10:15-12:00 p.m.	Work/school
12:00-1:00 p.m.	Lunch followed by brief silence and walk
1:00-5:00 p.m.	Work/school
5:00-5:30 p.m.	Meditation practice
5:30-7:00 p.m.	Dinner and interaction with family
7:00-10:00 p.m.	Light reading, TV, radio, evening walk, reading of spiritual literature, twelve-step meeting attendance
10:00 p.m.	Retire, brief prayer/meditation

and a vigorous walk to aid digestion. Your second meditation practice will come in early evening before supper. Digestion tends to interfere with the practice of meditation. If you can, resist the urge to do work-related activities in the evening. Instead, evening should be spent with the family or involved in light activities such as walking, watching TV, listening to the radio, or reading. It is best to retire at 10 p.m,. which is a window of opportunity. If you go to bed after 11 p.m. you may experience a "second wind," which can make it difficult to fall asleep. You may want to read a brief meditation or say your night prayers before retiring.

As much as you can, follow your daily schedule. Your mind and body will thrive on it. If you fall away from it you can gently come back to it. Do not force it. Do not neglect it (See D. F. Connell, 2003c).

Lesson 6

The Twelve Steps
and the Business of Recovery

WORKING THE TWELVE STEPS

Simply stated, the Twelve Steps of Alcoholics Anonymous are the most effective blueprint that we know for initiating and sustaining recovery from addictive diseases. The Twelve Steps provide us with both principles and a sequence of action steps to transform our lives completely: our personal and our occupational lives. The Twelve Steps provide both primary and secondary effects. The primary effect of the Twelve Steps is getting us sober. An important secondary effect is bringing a sense of serenity to our work life. The Twelve Steps are designed to produce serenity, equanimity, happiness, and balance in our personal and professional lives. You do not get sober simply to abstain from alcohol and drugs: you get sober to enjoy all that life has to offer and to become all you were born to be. This is the ultimate spiritual message and mission of the Twelve Steps.

The Twelve Steps provide essential guidance to help you navigate through recovery. This guidance is based on time-tested spiritual and psychological truths, which in turn lead to the development of a set of beliefs about how life works. Acquiring and internalizing recovery-based beliefs ultimately leads to a profound shift and a reorientation to a very different way of living life: a life of bliss, happiness, and freedom and a life free of the bondage of addiction. All recovering individuals, especially professionals, need a radical shift in orientation to how life works and how to live their lives. Why professionals

Managing Your Recovery from Addiction
© 2007 by The Haworth Press, Inc. All rights reserved.
doi:10.1300/5485_06

in particular? Because they are used to being "in charge," operating from a sense of ego power and getting results through intelligence, shrewdness, hard work, self-reliance, and a great amount of effort. These are all positive qualities, but they may be a hindrance to our recovery. The path of recovery requires a reorientation to a spiritual way of living life: a life based on relinquishing control to a higher power that is infinitely more powerful than the ego and limitless in its energy, scope, and manifestation. With a spiritual orientation you let go of control and ego. You realize that you are no longer in charge and move from a position of extreme independence to one of functional interdependence. You live a life based on power beyond your personality, ego, physical body, mind, emotions, and self-image.

Working the Twelve Steps and gaining a different orientation to life requires several things. First, it requires a sense of responsibility for who you are, where you are going, and how you are going to live your life. It also requires a sense of mindfulness. You approach the tasks of recovery with a gentle but persistent awareness of where you are and where you are going. The steps also require some effort— not the effort of pulling yourself up by your own bootstraps or the effort of controlling and micromanaging your life but the gentle effort of simply being with the Twelve Steps and working them on a daily basis.

Working the Twelve Steps also requires honesty and openness. The Twelve Steps call us to live genuine lives and require an interest in truth. The Twelve Steps are eternal, omnipresent, relentless truths that have worked since the dawn of humankind. Working the Twelve Steps also necessitates, as well as cultivates, a sense of self-love, love for God and for others and for the environment. Thus, a life of sobriety is a life of love.

This lesson is written for executives and professionals because in many ways you are more complex than others working the Twelve Steps. You are bright and believe you have more control and influence over life than you actually do. You believe your own press and you may even be a legend in your own mind. You may be perfectionist in your orientation to life, work too hard, and hide behind success. You are driven for reasons beyond your awareness. Many of you may even feel inwardly fraudulent, secretly fearing that if others really knew you and discovered your inner world, they would find that you are not what you project yourself to be. For much of your life you may have hidden behind a false sense of self or persona. You have convinced yourself even during your active addiction that everything is fine, that you are confident, adequate, and even superior. Many of you may have taken on the image of the executive or professional. This image is in and of itself fraudulent. The Twelve Steps dissolve this image and immerse you in a life of freedom and truth.

The following pages discuss the principles and practices of the Twelve Steps of Alcoholics Anonymous as they relate to executives and professionals. Although the Twelve Steps are universal in their scope and application, ultimately our interpretation of them and use of them in our daily lives is a personal experience. Professionals often have similar attitudes, beliefs, values, and orientations to life, and resonating with the Twelve Steps will bring peace both to the workplace and in your personal life.

Step One. We Admitted We Were Powerless over Alcohol— That Our Lives Had Become Unmanageable

The first step marks the beginning of our journey from the bondage of addiction to the freedom of recovery, and it begins with a disclosure, an admission. Admitting something may be difficult for us. In the workplace, for example, admitting a mistake can be construed as a threat to job stability and career advancement. When you make an admission, you take responsibility for something, but you also take a risk. If you admit that you have a feeling for someone, for example that you are attracted to or angry with him or her, you have to deal with the repercussions of your admission. If you tell someone that you are attracted to him or her, you open yourself up to the possibility that the attraction is not mutual and you may feel rejected. If you admit feelings of anger or envy to someone, you run the risk of being diminished in his or her view of you. An admission does have its risks, but it also has great rewards. In this case the reward is admission into a life of recovery.

An admission implies both a beginning and an ending, as well as a movement from one position to another. For example, if we are admitted into college, we end one style of life and begin another. We move on, we move out, and we move into a journey of learning. With the first step, in our admission of powerless over alcohol, we begin our journey of recovery.

The first step also asks us to be open and honest. We are admitting to our limitations. As addicts and alcoholics, we cannot control the use of alcohol or other drugs. With the first step we are honest about all the evidence in our lives that shows us that we are powerless over alcohol and other drugs. We are honest and open about the damage to our physical bodies, our family relationships, our friends and colleagues, and our work. We are open and honest about how alcohol and drugs controlled our lives, and about how while they did, we cared for little else. We are open about how we alienated others and ourselves. We did not fulfill our personal, family, and occupational responsibilities. With the first step we are open and honest and we become humble. We let go of our pride. We stop pretending. We stop covering up. We take a serious, penetrating look at our condition and acknowledge it.

Addiction is a disease of dyscontrol. With step one, we simply face upto the fact that we are not in control. We step back. We look at our life and ourselves objectively. We see the illusion of control. We realize that as addicts we never had control over alcohol and drug use, that it was only a matter of time until the full impact of this disease had its manifestation.

The first step also is a step out of a lonely, egocentric, isolated approach to life and into a life of community. ("We admitted . . .") We join other alcoholics and addicts on the journey of recovery. We stop going it alone.

Power

In step one we acknowledge our powerlessness over alcohol and drugs. This is a huge step for executives and professionals who, at least in the occupational sphere of their lives, often wield great power. Power implies control. To admit powerlessness over chemicals is to admit that we cannot control the use of chemicals. Most executives and professionals avoid any feeling that is remotely related to feeling powerless. Addiction, however, is a disease, and it does not respond to your willpower, your ego power, or your mind power. It is impervious to all of these. Despite feeling powerful and being powerful, we had no power over chemicals. Despite our best intentions, every time we drank or used drugs, we got into trouble. Despite our best intentions, we hurt people when we used alcohol or drugs. Despite our fierce devotion to our career, the ravages of addiction did not spare even that.

It is a well-known fact that with most executives and professionals, job performance is usually the last area of life to be affected by the deleterious impact of addiction. The job is usually the last thing to go. The rest of our lives may have been mess, but somehow we managed to continue to perform adequately at work, at least until the late stages of our disease. This continued feeling of "power" in the workplace reinforced our denial of addiction. Continuing to perform in the work place provided "proof" that we were not alcoholics or addicts. How could we be? We continued to do our job and do it well. However, if we take a closer look, even the illusion of power in the workplace began to deteriorate. For example, research studies have shown that more than 75 percent of newly sober executives report that their secretaries and administrative assistants conducted elaborate cover-up operations to camouflage their drinking or drug use. In addition, 60 percent of newly recovering executives say that their fellow executives protected them while they were drinking, And more than 90 percent of addicted executives and professionals state that they found it necessary to come in early, stay late or work on weekends to compensate for their diminished ability to get work done within normal working hours in the workplace. As addicts, we surrounded ourselves with professional enablers. This continued to reinforce our denial and help convince us that we were doing well when the fact was that we were slipping. Researchers have also identified something termed *job shrinkage*. Job shrinkage occurs when an impaired executive continues to do well in the workplace but actually does less and less as time goes on. He or she continues to perform adequately, or even in a superior way, but only on a diminishing list of projects. The job description of the executive addict begins to shrink, and eventually his or her waning competence is discovered.

"Pedestal professionals" such as dentists, doctors, lawyers, and engineers often share with business executives the same difficulty with step one. Professionals are extremely good at maintaining an illusion of adequacy, power, and even immunity from problems that affect everyone else such as addiction, mental illness, and physical problems. Professionals often are under the illusion that their education and experience will spare them the effects of addiction to alcohol and drugs. As we know, however, addiction is an equal-opportunity destroyer that will not respond to commodities such as power, prestige, intelligence, fame, notoriety, and money. Professionals may have an added obstacle to embracing step one because they feel that they are role models for the rest of society. Doctors are supposed after all, to be mentally and physically healthy. Lawyers are supposed to be sharp, intelligent, and in control. Scientists and engineers should somehow be able to use their intellect and scientific training to stave off addiction and mental health problems such as depression and anxiety. Of course, all of this is nonsense, but that does not stop professionals from being seduced into believing they somehow have a special status in life and can naturally transcend problems that plague us all.

Both professionals and businesspeople may also fear that they have a lot to lose by engaging in step one. Mostly this is a fear of loss: loss of prestige; loss of finances; loss of a license to practice medicine, law, or another profession; or loss of professional reputation. The alcoholic or addicted executive may fear loss of a career and may be concerned about the impact of his or her addiction on corporate functioning, health, and reputation. However, continuing to drink or drug is obviously not a solution to any of these losses. Working step one—that is, admitting our powerlessness over alcohol and drugs, admitting to our problem—essentially opens the way to solving the problem. So, the more fears we have of what we will lose through admitting to an addictive disease, the greater our willingness should be to come to such an admission, because through working the Twelve Steps we may be able to prevent or minimize all of the losses we fear will come about.

Manageability

With step one we admit our powerless over alcohol and other chemicals and we also admit that our lives had become unmanageable. Many executives and professionals spend their entire work lives devoted to managing: managing work, managing resources, managing people, managing information, even managing thoughts, feelings, and behaviors. Many executives and professionals are emotionally and psychologically controlled. They spend a lot of time and energy managing their emotional reactions in the workplace and even in personal and family life. Many executives and professionals are obsessed with details. They are meticulous managers of their daily schedule, exercise routine, diet, and extracurricular activities. All of this managing, however, began to break down as addiction progressed. However, that did not make the task of admitting unmanageability any easier. Good managers are in charge. They are organized. They are on top of the situation. They anticipate problems and preempt them if they can. They can be flexible and adaptable and can improvise in crisis management situations. The fact is, however, that all these management processes do not work with addiction. As an addict you do not manage your alcohol or drug use, it manages you. As the old AA adage goes, "First the man takes a drink, then the drink takes a drink, then the drink takes the man." Addiction takes over our lives until eventually, if it is untreated, no life is left to manage.

Face it: your addiction has made your life an uncontrollable mess. You are not managing anything anymore. Put your MBA and your scientific training aside and take a long, honest, penetrating look at the costs and consequences of your addiction. You have ruined your health, your mental health, your marriage, your relationship with your children, and perhaps your job. You are definitely experiencing a state of unmanageability due to this disease. You are facing a management problem that you probably were not trained to address at business school. However, you do not have to give up entirely on the concept of management, except as it applies to your disease. You can engage in management of sorts in recovery. We might call it *participative management*. You may need to "outsource" for some help. You need a coach. You need a consultant. You need a different kind of management and way to manage. You need the management of recovery that can come from a relationship with a higher power and that comes with engaging in step two of the Twelve Steps.

However, before we move onto that, take some time to look for evidence of powerlessness and unmanageability in your life as a result of your addiction. Do some digging into the past. Get a sense of your history during your active addiction. You can review your personnel and performance record on your job. Review your legal history. Look at hospital and doctor bills. Look at your finances. Review your social history. Who did you say what to and what were the effects during your active addiction? Did you have any car wrecks? How has your behavior during periods when you were drinking or drugging affected your marital relationship or your relationship with your kids? List concrete examples of how your addiction has affected your family life, your work life, and your social activities. How many hobbies and other activities have you let go because of your addiction? Look at all the ways your life has changed over the course of your addiction up to the present. Simply put, look for any and all evidence of unmanageability, disorganization, and chaos in your life due to your addiction.

Step Two. Came to Believe that a Power Greater Than Ourselves Could Restore Us to Sanity

Working step two introduces us to life beyond the ego, beyond our identity, beyond our personality, beyond the mind, and beyond simple willpower. As an executive or professional, this may be very difficult for you to conceive. You have been living an egocentric life. You have become more and more selfish as your addiction has progressed. But is your ego the only thing going on in life? Is the ego not connected to the rest of humanity? Are you not a part of nature and ultimately a part of the universe? It is time to get reconnected to the power source of all that is.

Being an executive or professional can make for a lonely life, especially if you are a CEO or in a leadership position. The same goes for a doctor, dentist, or psychologist in private practice. You are it. You are the professional. You go it alone. This can be overwhelming to any ego, so the ego sets up defenses and pretends that it is more powerful and influential than it actually is. The reality is that the ego does not control life, cannot control life, and never did. There are simply too many variables interacting at any given time for the ego to manage life. Without your knowing it, your ego is actually connected to a higher self or higher power. Your ego gets its power, energy, direction, intelligence, and awareness from a higher power. Without a higher power, the ego could not exist, nor could your body. It would shrink and curl up as to a dry leaf does in late fall. It simply makes infinite sense to reconnect you with your power source. Actually you have never been disconnected from it—only apparently disconnected.

You have simply been unaware of the infinite power that runs your life and runs the universe.

Our higher power is omnipresent. It is always there, it always has been there, and it always will be there. It is not subject to time and space. It is not time bound or restricted to any one location in the universe. The problem is we simply overlook our higher power as the source of our life. With step two, we are similar to a small drop of water rejoining the ocean. We reclaim our connection with our divine birthright. Realizing our connection to our higher power is the beginning of the process of spiritual awakening and spiritual realization. Here we begin to relinquish control over our lives to the ultimate controller. We step outside of our own willpower. We allow divine power to infuse itself into every thought, action, and experience in our life. With this relinquishing of control, hope begins to dawn. We begin to see the possibility of a new style of functioning of a new life. Addiction has led to profound disorganization, disrepair, and loss in our life. We have lost so much due to our addiction. Addiction has so distorted our emotions, thoughts, and behaviors that we could describe our lives as insane. By reconnecting with our higher power, a state of stability, serenity, and sanity begins to dawn in our life.

As a result of the insanity of our addiction, we have lost our connection with ourselves and with God, as we understand Him. This is a connection that we did have as a child. Perhaps we got it through the religion we were raised with. The word "religion" comes from the Latin *religire,* which means "to relink" or "to reconnect." Religion is about reconnecting with God or our higher power. As mentioned in the previous lesson, the word "spirituality" comes from the Latin *spiritus,* meaning "breath" or "breathing." Spirituality is about the breath of our higher power infused into our life. We can utilize both our religion and our spirituality to wake up again to our divine power source. This reconnection involves stepping outside of our professional persona or identity. Executives and professionals develop a work persona that can eventually become their sole identity. This is a psychological trap that we must transcend. Our identity is actually boundless and beyond any particular personality or persona we take on in life. Letting go of our professional identity can be a scary process. However, it can also be a relief because letting go means that we gain something much more powerful and expansive.

Working step two involves a reorientation to the spiritual as opposed to the material dimension of life. We now redirect our thinking and our awareness to our higher power. We are patient with ourselves. We give ourselves time to immerse ourselves in the experience of our higher power. We let go, we give, in and we allow the healing power of our reconnection with our higher power to take over our lives. In working step two, devote time to spiritual reflection and introspection. It is time to realize that you need help. It is time to let go of the fierce self-reliance that has driven your career. It is time to let go of the illusion of independence that is common in U.S. society. We need to realize that we are interdependent, that we need others and they need us. Challenge your notion of independence and self-reliance. Who made the clothes that you are wearing? Who built the house that you live in? Who took care of you when you fell ill? Who made the roads that you drive on when you go to work? Others did all this for us. We need every single person on this planet. As Dr. Deepak Chopra, has stated, "There are no spare parts in the universe." (Personal Communication, Chopra, 1992). We all have a role to play, and we are all needed. You need others. You need this program. You need a higher power. You need to read this manual. You are not independent. You cannot artificially separate yourself from the rest of the universe. Forget about that. It is time to trust in the process, to trust in the universe. Most of life is beyond our awareness. If you are having difficulty with the idea of God or a higher power, think of all the wonderful physiological processes—billions of them—that are going on right now in your body. You do not know how it all works, but you do know that it does work. You do know that intelligence and an awareness is orchestrating the whole process. This is the higher power. Embrace it.

The experience of your higher power is often more poignant when you are in a group situation because the group provides a "collective consciousness" in which you can experience yourself in recovery. Interestingly, some impressive scientific research has been conducted on the power of prayer and meditation in group situations. Coming together at a Twelve Step meeting, group therapy, or another gathering synergistically increases the power of prayer and meditation and their benefits. Prayer, meditation, and spiritual practices introduce coherence into chaotic situations. So, in working step two, reconnect with God, and reconnect with others. Seek out sober people. Enjoy their purity of consciousness. Collaborate with them and enlist their assistance. Turn your life over to the process of life itself.

To help you work step two, engage in activities that promote awareness of the smallness and insignificance of your ego. Visit Rocky Mountain National Park in Colorado. Spend some time in the high peaks. Go to the Grand Canyon. Visit a monastery or a convent. Talk to a chaplain at a hospital who spends a great deal of time with dying individuals. Walk through a cemetery. Realize the transience of the life of the physical body and, therefore, the ego. Read a book on quantum physics. Study the concepts of eternity and infinity, which is the realm of the higher power. Start to think big. Expand your awareness beyond your present situation. A new life awaits you now, an infinitely expansive life, and a life in recovery. Be grateful for God. Be grateful for a second chance at life.

Step Three. Made a Decision to Turn Our Will and Our Lives over to the Care of God, As We Understood Him

In working step three, we allow our spiritual nature to manifest itself, to emerge from dormancy and inactivity, and to infuse itself into our conscious life. Despite what you might think, this should be an effortless, easy, natural process. It is not something that we can make happen. Why? Because the spiritual is the essence of our nature. As the great Jesuit priest, mystic, and evolutionary biologist Teilhard de Chardin said, "We are not physical beings having a spiritual experience, we are spiritual beings having a physical experience." The ultimate dimension of our lives is the spiritual. It is the realm of the divine, of God, of the higher power. Allow this realm to become predominant in you life. Although we cannot force this to happen, we can make a decision to make a turn toward the spiritual. We make an informed decision based on the first two steps we have completed. In the third step, our training in problem solving and decision making can come into play. We make our decision to turn toward God based on our thoughts, experiences, and analysis in steps one and two. It makes sense to turn our lives over to God because during active addiction, we really screwed up our lives. Here we want to recapture our lives. During an active addiction our lives were given over to an addictive disease. With this step we make a decision to go in an entirely different direction.

How do we do this? We simply and effortlessly align ourselves with the infinite power that runs through all of life. We engage in a spiritual collaboration and merger. We do not have to create God or a higher power; we simply have to get out of our own way, that is, get out of the ego's way and allow our higher power to emerge. It will do so as naturally as sap rises through the stems and leaves of a plant. It is a completely natural, effortless process. When the clouds block the sun, is the sun gone? Do we have to create sunlight in order for it to be bright again? No. We allow the winds to blow the clouds away and the sun emerges in all its luminosity. It has always been there, it will always be there, and it is the power source of life on Earth.

The truth is we have never been separate from God or our higher power. The separation has been an apparent one. As a great spiritual teacher said, "There is one thing God cannot do—he cannot separate himself from the soul." As Ralph Trine said, "In essence, the life of God and the life of man are identically the same and so are one. They differ not in essence, in quality; they differ in degree."

The God aspect of AA can be difficult for recovering individuals, especially executives and professionals. Many patients ask us how we, the Authors would define God. Eliphas Levi described God as "A single spirit that fills infinity." God can be described as pure love, as ultimate power. It is difficult to conceive of God through the intellect. It has been said that "God is concealed from the mind but revealed in the heart." We sense God. We intuit God. We feel God. We like Empedocles' definition of God: "God is a circle whose center is everywhere and whose circumference nowhere." Ultimately we must all have a personal experience of and define God in our own way, as we understand Him. However daunting, this is a wonderful endeavor and well worth the effort. Once you become intimate with God and experience a divine presence, life is never the same again.

As indicated, step three involves a decision-making process. In psychology and management the distributive theory of leadership says that anyone in a given group or organization has leadership skills that they can contribute to the group. Following this theory as executives and professionals, we relinquish our need to run the show and delegate authority to our collaborator, in this case the ultimate collaborator, our higher power. This is the way out of the bondage of addiction. This is the move from isolation to intimacy and union. During active addiction we have become spiritually vapid and dry. When we allow God now to care for us, we reverse all of this. As mentioned, executives and professionals are deficient at self-care. This is an extremely important step because we are now letting God care for us. The implied dependency here may be difficult for you, but it is important to allow others, particularly God, to do things for us. With this step we cultivate a sense of receptivity. We give up and give over, and in so doing we make the ultimate investment in ourselves. We let go of ourself and we allow the healing, caring processes inherent in life to predominate. With this step we reorient to a spiritual way of being. We reclaim our infinite inner power by aligning ourselves with the ultimate power.

The research on spirituality and spiritual practices such as prayer and meditation shows us that a turn toward the spiritual life has tremendous implications for our physical and mental health (O'Connell, 2003b). As indicated in the lesson in this book on managing spirituality, introducing God and spirituality into our lives can literally be life-saving. It can shrink the plaque in our arteries. It can lower our blood pressure. It can produce good cardiovascular health. It can relieve depression, anxiety, and other disorders of mood. It can change our personality for the better. It can raise our IQ. It can sharpen our senses and perceptions. It can reduce stress hormones in our body and make our brain waves coherent. In general, the effects of spirituality are exactly the opposite of those of an addictive disease. It just makes plain good sense to turn our will and lives over to the care of God. We have screwed up our lives. It is time to drop all that and allow the intelligence that runs the universe to run our lives.

It is time for a change in management and leadership! This way, we will stay alive and flourish. It is important for you to realize that you do not now, nor have you ever, run the show in life. You do not know what creates the thoughts in your mind or what beats your heart or even how it is done. Ninety-nine percent of life goes on mysteriously through processes that are out of your awareness and understanding. You cannot control your life; you can only influence it. With a turn toward God we become process oriented and we let go of goals, objectives, and outcomes. We stay in the moment and go along for the ride. With step three we stop micromanaging our lives—and what a relief that is!

Step Four. Made a Searching and Fearless Moral Inventory of Ourselves

Working step four involves taking a serious, penetrating look at ourselves. It is time to stop fooling around. It is time to stop kidding ourselves. It is time to drop our ego defenses, look ourselves squarely in the eye, and tell it like it is, as we used to say in the Sixties. In many ways, this is no different from an objective, logical analysis of any problem in the workplace. Corporations take inventory all the time. Managers and industrial psychologists all engage in organizational analysis to help detect problems, define them, and gather data to set up an action plan to address and resolve them. This kind of objective, detached, cool, scientific approach can be applied to step four. Forget how you feel about yourself and simply take an objective, rational look at yourself. Accept yourself at your absolute worst.

When you are working step four, let go of any fears you have about what you might see and its supposed implications for your life. Forget about interpreting and commenting on what you did during your active addiction, which may induce a sense of guilt, shame, or compunction. Now is not the time for judgments, criticisms, interpretations, and cognitive elaborations of your problems with character, dysfunctional behaviors, feelings, and emotions during your active addiction. It is important to really let go here. It is a platitude in psychology that "what we resist persists." Our dysfunctional behavior and feelings during our active addiction only work to promote confusion in our lives. It is time to replace confusion with clarity, and this is accomplished through embracing and working the fourth step. Here we identify our defects of character. We bring them to light. We look at them objectively, and through this process we become intimate with ourselves again. This is very important for executives and professionals. Executives are typically "other" focused. They pay very little attention to themselves. They are constantly concerned with others—the family, the corporation, the government, the press, employees, the customer, the bottom line, etc. Step four involves an exclusive focus on the self, on you.

When you are working the fourth step, be honest, direct, open, and concrete. Write down everything that you saw, felt, and experienced during your active addiction that involved hurt to yourself and others.

Stop kidding yourself. Stop making things more palatable to you. Everybody has a dark side. It is time to embrace it. In the back of your mind realize that all of your dysfunctional behavior during active addiction is changeable. No, it is true you cannot turn back the clock, but you can change your behaviors now. With this step we deal with the past. We look at an inventory of our lives. It is a good idea to repeat the fourth step several times during early recovery. We have found that each time you do it, you begin to reclaim more and more of yourself and you begin to build greater and greater levels of honesty, openness, and self-transparency.

Completing the fourth step can lead to a profound sense of exhilaration, freedom, and relief. It is true that "the truth will set you free." The fourth step is a personal accounting. Sit down with pencil or pen in hand and simply do it. It is time to take stock, to take inventory. Approach it as you would any business task. It is time to take care of business.

Step Five. Admitted to God, to Ourselves, and to Another Human Being the Exact Nature of Our Wrongs

It is a truism in psychology that we are "only as sick as our secrets." It is time to stop being secretive. Carrying around secrets is a great psychological burden and comes with an enormous psychological price tag. It takes more energy to hold in and cover up a secret than to let it go. However, telling our deep dark secrets is counterintuitive and against every addictive impulse that we have. That is exactly why the Twelve Steps ask us to do it. It is said in India in the study of yoga that one of the most cleansing things that has to transpire in yoga study is to tell all of your secret thoughts to at least one person during the course of your training. Letting go of secrets and admitting wrongdoings is extremely purifying and clarifying. It is a kind of ego detoxification, and it resolves deep shame and guilt. Psychologically, admitting wrongdoings reduces egocentricity, narcissism, and pride. These are all characteristics of the executive personality we can afford to reduce and/or eliminate!

Step five involves a reaching outside of ourselves. We reach out to others, we reach out to God, and we reach out to the part of ourself that is healthy, rational, loving, and wants us to be free. Through step five we free ourselves from the shackles of the past. We complete a mental housecleaning and, in the process of completing step five, a shift to another style of functioning, the shift from addiction to recovery. Through step five we expose ourselves to ourselves, to our higher power, and to at least one other person. We do not have to hide anymore. It may be embarrassing, it may be anxiety arousing, it may be humiliating, but ultimately none of this matters. The only thing that matters is freedom.

For executives and professionals, particularly those who work within a corporation, this type of behavior and activity is extremely counterintuitive. In the workplace, we often subscribe to a "cover-up" philosophy. We never admit to a wrongdoing. We cover our tracks. We camouflage our weaknesses. We never let them see us sweat! We fix on a poker face. We downplay any weaknesses or imperfections. This may be appropriate in the workplace, but we have to drop this orientation when we do step five.

You can do your step five in the context of a counseling or psychotherapy session. You can do it with your sponsor or with someone else you trust and respect. It is best to choose someone who has been through the fifth step many times, someone who understands recovery and the value of Twelve Steps work. It may be advisable to complete the fifth step soon after you complete your fourth step since the fifth step is an important element in the healing process. After you complete your fifth step take some time for yourself. Be nice to yourself. Perhaps go on a spiritual retreat. Engage in a pleasurable activity. Get lots of rest. It can be exhausting and draining doing a fifth step. After you complete it you may want to begin a new activity or project that can symbolize the death of your life in active addiction and a rebirth to a life of sobriety.

Step Six. We're Entirely Ready to Have God Remove All These Defects of Character

By completing steps four and five, we have begun a transformation and we continue it in this step. Here we prepare ourselves to have our infinite higher power purify all the distortions, convolutions, and imperfections in our nature. As a psychologist carrying out a lot of psychotherapy, I have realized that it is nearly impossible to reduce or eliminate character problems, or any other problem for that matter, solely through psychological means. We cannot deal with problems of the mind on the level of the mind! We need a higher power. We need to get to subtler, more refined levels of our subjective inner life, and that means we need to go directly to the spiritual dimension, the foundation of our lives. The practice of meditation, in particular, develops a sense of receptivity, innocence, and nongrasping, nonclinging awareness that is necessary to allow a higher power to emerge and cleanse mind and body. This step is about preparing for such a cleansing. This step is about getting ready to do the work of completing a transformation. To prepare for it, review your fourth step inventory. Get ready to identify and let go of self-defeating behaviors that emerged in your addiction. Pray to God or your higher power for a sense of willingness. Be patient; take your time. Begin to look at your self-defeating behaviors and attitudes. Ask yourself why you acted the way you did. Ask what these behaviors did for you. What were their benefits and limitations? Look at what fears were behind your self-defeating behaviors and character defects. What motivated them? What have you avoided by engaging in self-defeating behaviors?

As you learned in the executive group, addicts often have personality problems that predate addiction and are amplified and exaggerated by addiction. In addition, the neurotoxic effects of alcohol and drugs of abuse themselves produce personality and character problems. Character defects typically emerge early in the addictive process, when they are mild in their severity. As addiction progresses, they become worse and worse. Early signs of character problems are discomfort in intimate relationships, oversensitivity to rejection, growing feelings of shame and inadequacy, growing fears of being alone or abandoned, an increase in conflict in relationships, difficulty with managing emotions, distancing ourselves from family members and close friends, a growing sense of self-centeredness, and the development of self-sabotaging, self-defeating, self-destructive behaviors (Fields and Vandenbelt, 2003). Others may see us becoming increasingly angry, arrogant, boorish, contemptuous, cynical, dishonest, grandiose, greedy, insecure, intolerant, perfectionist, and self-pitying. Character defects such as these typically grow in intensity and frequency as addiction progresses.

Completing step six can involve interviewing others on how we have changed as our addiction has progressed. This will help us get a more complete, well-rounded experience of our personality, character, and behavior problems. Once we get a pretty good picture of our psychological and emotional profile, it is time to let go. It is time to allow our higher power gently to emerge and to purify, clarify, and dissolve our defects of character. The wonderful thing about step six is that we do not have to do anything. We just have to get out of the way and allow the natural processes inherent in our infinite higher power to do all the work. This is the promise of salvation. It is easy. It is effortless. As the Bible says, "Ask and it shall be given you." Ask your higher power to emerge, and then allow the process to happen.

Step Seven. Humbly Asked Him to Remove Our Shortcomings

Step seven is engaging in prayer, a prayer of asking God or your higher power, with a sense of humility, to take away our shortcomings. For executives and professionals, asking for anything is difficult. After all, we are supposed to do it ourselves. We are in charge, we are the leaders, and we are the bottom line. Many of us have been used to going it alone in life. We are not supposed to need help. We are supposed to give help. We do not need advice and guidance; we give it. Admitting that you need help and cannot do something by yourself is a major step for executives and professionals, as is the ability to accept help and be receptive to help from others—in this case, your higher power. Remember, you cannot do it all. You do need help. You need the help of the steps, the help of your higher power, and the help of others. Allow yourself to accept help. Let go of your pride. Let go of your egotism. Realize your shortcomings and allow your higher power to rise up through your awareness and purify all the distortions and defects you have acquired during your active addiction.

Step Eight. Made a List of All Persons We Had Harmed and Became Willing to Make Amends to Them All

In working step eight, we deepen our experience of spirituality and get ready and willing to let go of and heal the past for others and ourselves. With step eight we ask for forgiveness. It is extremely important to ask for forgiveness in life. When you hurt someone, you create an imbalance. You have to restore balance if you are to have peace and serenity. It is a kind of spiritual and psychological economic principle. With step eight we balance our lives again. We fix the damage we have done. Addiction is a damaging, horrible disease that cruelly affects those with whom the addict interacts. In step eight, we can go back to step four and from that list write down the name of each and every person we have harmed during our active addiction. We construct a comprehensive list. We list not only those to whom we did horrible things but also those to and for whom we did not do things: those whom we neglected, ignored, or alienated because of our active addiction. With step eight we use prayer and our talk to God or our higher power to make amends. When it is feasible, we also make a plan to make amends physically to those whom we have hurt. Through our addiction we have damaged our connection to others. It is time to restore that connection. It is time to get over our embarrassment and our shame and prepare ourselves to do the necessary work of healing by making up for our damaging behavior and by asking forgiveness for it. With step eight we become ready and willing, and in step nine we perform the necessary actions.

Step Nine. Made Amends to Such People Whenever Possible, Except When to Do So Would Injure Them or Others

In working step nine we begin to repair damage. This is a restoration step. We rebuild, replenish, refurbish, and reconfigure our lives. With step nine we personally seek out the people whom we have hurt. We tell them what we have done and why it happened, and we ask them how we can balance the scales with them. How can we make it up to them? How can we make it right? This is a step of taking ownership and responsibility for your behavior during your active addiction. Some of us subscribe to the belief that you never look back. But with step nine, looking back is exactly what we do. One last time we revisit the past and we attempt to make things right. If we have stolen money from someone, we give it back. If we cut out of work early from an employer, we work overtime for them. If we cannot comfortably or feasibly give back to someone from whom we have taken money, we can give money to a charity or donate time to a charity. Always a way can be found to make amends. Finally, if we cannot physically make amends, we can pray to our higher power to help heal the person we have damaged, who may be deceased or unavailable.

To prepare for this step, it is best to go over step eight and discuss it with your sponsor, a recovery mentor, or a close friend. Discuss your strategy for making apologies, cash payments, or making amends through a telephone call or written letter. Get a lot of support before you set out on step nine. You may even want to take some friends from the program with you to give you courage and support. Let go of your shame and embarrassment. This is a healing step. It is taking a risk. Others may be mad at us or extremely grief stricken because of our behavior during active addiction. We need to accept any emotional reaction we get from others. You may want to role-play with some program friends your personal discussions with those to whom you are going to make amends. This can reduce performance anxiety. If the people whom you have hurt are still in your life, resolve to be attentive to their needs. Be responsible to them. Show up on time. Be considerate of them. Do things for them that need to be done. Continue to admit your wrongdoings and continue to restore and repair the relationship when it becomes damaged. Finally, if you think your encounter with a person you harmed during your active addiction will itself be a psychologically damaging experience, do not make amends in person. Rather, do it through your relationship with a higher power by prayer and aspirations.

Step Ten. Continued to Take Personal Inventory and When We Were Wrong Promptly Admitted it

Working this step reminds us that recovery is an ongoing process and not simply an outcome to be achieved or a static goal to be realized. Similar to continuous quality improvement within a corporation, step ten reminds us that the road to recovery is always under repair. Recovery requires continuous maintenance. As we progress in recovery we continually grow and develop. This is the nature of life. Step ten keeps us oriented toward this continual growth and keeps us going in the direction of recovery from moment to moment in our lives. Step ten helps us maintain the gains that we have made and to continue them on a daily basis through careful attention and action when necessary. We can engage in step ten works several times throughout the day by turning things over to our higher power and being mindful of working a recovery program, especially during times of great stress and conflict. Step ten involves constant self-monitoring and self-care and is a useful step to offset complacency and character defects that may get reactivated, such as grandiosity, narcissism, self-centeredness, and self-importance. It is inevitable that some of these qualities will creep back into our program. We need a continual weeding of the garden to keep them under control. Working step ten continually builds self-confidence and sense of competence at recovery. It also infuses a sense of humility. We become quite accustomed to admitting mistakes and taking responsibility for our lives.

The tenth step keeps us mindful and in the moment. Cognitive therapy tells us that our first reaction to a stressful or conflict situation is almost always wrong—it is irrational, dysfunctional, and maladaptive. In working the tenth step it is important to take on board the idea "when in doubt, delay." Do not react impulsively to every stressful situation in recovery. Get into the habit of taking a step back, taking stock, taking inventory, engaging in a microanalysis of the stressful event or conflict situation, and then taking more considered, level-headed action.

It is best to do a quick tenth step in the morning and in the evening before we go to bed. Of course, we can take it several times during the day, especially difficult days. The tenth step reminds us that recovery and sobriety are a moment-to-moment affair, as life is.

Step Eleven. Sought Through Prayer and Meditation to Improve Our Conscious Contact with God, As We Understood Him, Praying Only for Knowledge of His Will for Us and the Power to Carry That Out

As indicated in the lesson on managing spirituality, meditation, prayer, and contemplative practices are the technologies that restructure and reconfigure the nervous system to support a spiritual awakening and a spiritual life in recovery. The emerging field of neurotheology shows us that prayer and meditation have powerful effects on the brain and central nervous system as well as a tremendous impact in terms of enhancing physical and mental health. The regular practice of meditation leads to the introduction of a balanced, integrated style of functioning for the nervous system. It produces this through the healing silence of meditation that activates the homeostatic repair mechanisms in the body to heal physical and mental damage, which leads to a sense of good health, well-being, serenity, and happiness. The practice of prayer profoundly reorients our awareness to the spiritual dimension of life and has its own good-health-bestowing benefits. Ultimately, prayer leads to an intensification of our intimacy with God or our higher power and a feeling of divine unity. As the last part of this step reminds us, prayer is not about ego fulfillment. Prayer is about God's will. As St. Niluss said, "We should never pray to God that he may grant what we desire, but that his will may be accomplished in us." Prayer is mindful attention to God. It refines our nervous system and cultures and cultivates a spiritual style of functioning. Through regular prayer and meditation, the feeling of unseen hands and forces guiding us through life begins to grow.

Prayer and meditation are absolutely essential in recovery and form the heart of the eleventh step. How important are these spiritual practices? Consider this quotation from no less a spiritual luminary than the Buddha: "This is the only way . . . to explain existence, to overcome sadness and grievances, to banish death and misery, to find the right path, to realize nirvana—it is correct meditation." Meditation is a wonderful way to purify the mind of addictive thinking. As Joan Borysenko said, "Meditation helps keep us from identifying with the movies of the mind." Meditation helps us to disengage from dysfunctional, addictive thinking. During meditation we may experience a suspension of thoughts as the mind is quieted and stilled. Meditation is serenity itself.

We take a very practical approach to the eleventh step. You should begin and end each day with meditation and prayer and stop several times during the day for mini prayer and meditation sessions. Most of the major world religions encourage this. For example, in traditional Judaism, we are instructed to pray three times a day. Catholic monastic traditions urge us to have a sacred pause seven times a day. Islam calls its followers to pray five times throughout the day. It is clear that prayer and meditation lead to a lasting state of serenity and happiness. Follow the instructions in the lesson on managing spirituality. Look at prayer and meditation as intimate communication with God. Develop a mindset of loving, respectful attention as you would with any loved one. Do not be concerned with how to pray and meditate. Just open your heart and mind to God and ask God to reveal himself to you. Realize that God wants to know all about you. He is vitally interested in your life. As St. Augustine said about God, "You have made us for yourself." Through prayer and meditation, God reclaims you. Through daily prayer and meditation we live continually in God's presence. Sounds wonderful, does it not?

Step Twelve. Having Had a Spiritual Awakening As a Result of These Steps, We Try to Carry This Message to Alcoholics and to Practice These Principles in All of Our Affairs

In working the twelfth step we realize an eternal spiritual truth—in order to really get something, we have to give it away. Not only that, but the giver gets back a thousandfold whatever he or she has given. The twelfth step is a service step. We serve others. Through working the Twelve Steps we have become transformed. We now have something to give others! The twelfth step is really all of the Twelve Steps' principles and practices in action. Through the twelfth step we embody and manifest all that is the Twelve Steps of AA. Through working the twelfth step we become, as St. Francis put it, "An instrument of God's peace." We become a conduit for the divine. We become the higher power in action. The twelfth step is an example of what has been known for centuries in India as Bakti yoga. This is a system of spiritual advancement with its main focus on selfless service to others. This in and of itself can transform our lives and catapult us to great spiritual heights.

With the twelfth step we move out of ourselves and into the world. We give something away to others because we can give it away and we have something to give now. We practice Twelve Steps principles continually in our lives, especially in the workplace and at home. We have become spiritually transformed. We have become sober and we realize that we have something to give humankind. We have a purpose in life. Our lives have meaning. As the great scientist and spiritual educator Dr. Deepak Chopra put it, "There are no spare parts in the universe." We are important! We have a purpose, and from now on our lives are about fulfilling this purpose. Through working the twelfth step we become acutely aware of all the misery, especially the misery caused by active addiction. We become compassionate. Our hearts swell with empathy and love. We become a conduit for hope for those still in the grips of active addiction, and it feels so good to give to others! How do we do this? We go early to meetings and make coffee. We introduce ourselves to newcomers and help them become integrated into the program. We practice wonderful qualities such as patience, tolerance, forgiveness, politeness, and consideration. We provide rides to meetings at counseling centers and other sites to those who need them. We become public speakers and we speak up about the wonderful process of recovery, both formally and informally. We introduce AA meetings at our workplace. We join the underground "Friends of Bill W." We become silently present to all those alcoholics who need our help, and through the practice of the twelfth step we realize what life and sobriety are all about—love in action.

CONCLUSION

In business the bottom line is profit. In recovery the bottom line is sobriety. In the business of recovery, working and reworking the Twelve Steps on a continual basis leads to a profitable life in the widest sense of the term. It simply makes immense sense to work the Twelve Steps. They keep you sober, and without your sobriety you will not have success in business or with your family. You will not have your good health; indeed, you may even lose your life. Working the twelve steps is an investment in yourself, an investment that will bring infinite returns. The Twelve Steps are practices and principles you can apply in nearly every situation in life—certainly including your profession and in the workplace. In approaching your job and profession, absorb and utilize twelve-step practices and principles in your day-to-day activities. An article in *Harvard Business Review* reported that we spend 49 percent of our lives in the workplace. Indeed, the workplace presents the greatest opportunities for growth, development, and advancement in sobriety as well as some of the greatest threats and risks for our recovery. How we negotiate our professional lives as well as our personal lives is a vital recovery process.

I urge you to read and reread this lesson often, especially during the first year of your recovery. Find ways you can apply the information in this lesson to your daily life. Read other books, pamphlets, and resources on the Twelve Steps. Yes, recovery requires work, but as one great spiritual teacher put it, "We work to become, not to acquire." Through working the Twelve Steps we experience the transformation to become all we were born to be.

Lesson 7

A Refresher Course
in Addictions Treatment

The inpatient, or an intensive outpatient, treatment experience gives the chemically dependent individual essential knowledge, behavioral skills, and emotional, psychological, and spiritual experiences that are considered to be fundamental to the task of ongoing recovery from addictive diseases. Returning again and again to the knowledge that you acquired during the laying of the foundation for your recovery can be very useful, especially during the first year of recovery. We cannot fully replicate your inpatient experience. There you may have experienced a profound sense of safety, the sanctuary of an enlightened community of patients and therapists who stewarded you toward sobriety. We know you cannot get the intimacy and exhilaration of your therapy group by reading a lesson on the basics of addictions recovery. However, we believe that this lesson will reactivate and reinforce the many important issues and experiences you gained during your recovery foundation.

This lesson is a refresher course on the basics of addictions treatment, a form of "Addictions Treatment 101." We consider this information absolutely essential for anyone in recovery. We extrapolate a huge amount of information from a variety of psychological and addiction resources and present it here. Periodically, you can reread this lesson to reinforce all that you have learned about recovery thus far. You may find it extremely beneficial as you progress through the tasks of early, middle, and late recovery.

Managing Your Recovery from Addiction
© 2007 by The Haworth Press, Inc. All rights reserved.
doi:10.1300/5485_07

WORKING STEPS ONE, TWO, AND THREE

Step One

Addressing step one marks the beginning of your treatment. In step one we admit that we were powerless over alcohol and drugs and that our lives have become unmanageable. Step one helps us gain a greater understanding of our powerlessness over chemicals, of the process of unmanageability, and of the role of surrender and acceptance in recovery. As our addiction progresses, it affects every aspect of our lives. We experience unmanageability and lack of control physically, mentally, spirituality, legally, socially, etc. We thought we had control of our alcohol and drug use, but all we had really was the illusion of control. The defense of massive denial makes it nearly impossible to accept lack of control over alcohol and drugs. Psychological denial, at least for a brief period, protected us from feeling the consequences of the disease of addiction.

With step one we surrender to our lack of control over alcohol and drugs and we accept our powerlessness, admitting utter defeat in the face of addiction. The exact wording of step one is "We admitted we were powerless over alcohol—that our lives have become unmanageable." This step is deliberately worded with the pronoun "we." You can take this to mean that you are not alone. You do not work a program of recovery in isolation. As the saying goes, "I get drunk, we stay sober." Addressing step one helps us break through our denial and accept the reality of addiction. It is a hard reality to accept, but it is the most important recovery task that we have. If we do not accept it, we may die. Working step one helps us become willing to change the attitudes, beliefs, and behaviors that kept our addiction in place. Working it helps us open the door to accepting help from others. Completing step one is discovering the truth about our lives, about our disease. Through completion of step one we acknowledge that addiction is a chronic, progressive, incurable, and potentially fatal disease. Complete Worksheet 7.1 to begin considering these issues.

Step Two

In working step two we gain a greater insight into the chaos and confusion that accompanied our addiction. We understand the differ-

WORKSHEET 7.1. Working Step One

Loss of Control

In the space below review your behavior during your active addiction. Write down the age that you began using chemicals, the specific chemicals you used, the amounts, how frequently you used them, and your duration of use. Pay particular attention to how your drug and alcohol use progressed.

Now think about times when you were out of control with alcohol and drug use. In the space below write down specific times when you vowed not to use alcohol and/or drugs and used them anyway. Also include times when you used alcohol and drugs *more* than you intended to. Pay particular attention to periods in your life when you experienced brownouts and blackouts, periods of amnesia, and serious consequences of drinking, such as severe withdrawal experiences, serious accidents, seizures, and comas.

(continued)

(continued)

Unmanageability

The unmanageability associated with your addiction affected every area of your life. In the space below write down some examples of the various types of unmanageability associated with addiction.

Emotional Unmanageability (uncontrolled moods, fears, outbursts, depression, sadness, confusion, and other negative emotions)

Spiritual Unmanageability (having no sense of peace, no purpose in life, loss of self-respect, inability to give or receive love, feelings of alienation from God)

Family Unmanageability (lying, manipulation, and hurting family members)

Sexual Unmanageability (promiscuity, sexual diseases, poor performance)

(continued)

(continued)

   Intellectual Unmanageability (memory loss, disorganization, memory problems, poor problem solving, failing in school, abandonment of intellectual pursuits)

   Social Unmanageability (lying to and manipulating our friends, betraying them, losing friends)

   Financial Unmanageability (money spent on drugs or lost due to drug and alcohol use, financial opportunities lost due to addiction)

   Physical Unmanageability (medical problems, poor health, dental problems, injuries, accidents, poor nutrition)

How have things changed?

   In the following space list the benefits of your recovery program and how they have balanced the consequences of addictive alcohol and drug use.

ence between our ego and your higher power and get a sense of the role of spirituality in recovery and of the role and function of your higher power in bringing it about.

Step Two reads, "Came to believe that a power greater than ourselves could restore us to sanity." What is insanity? It is not necessarily being crazy, psychiatrically disturbed, or out of our minds. Acting insanely can simply be doing the same thing, the same way, over and over again, and getting the same negative consequences while expecting different results. Addiction can bring on a form of insanity.

Step two provides an antidote to our self-centeredness during active addiction. We were only concerned with one thing, that is, drinking and drugging. Step two is realizing that a higher power exists and understanding that something greater than our ego easily restores our lives to serenity. We realize that we do not have to fix the problem. We just have to get out of the way and allow our higher power to restore us to our original nature before addiction ruined our lives. When we get a serious disease, such as addiction, or cancer, or heart disease, we may ask ourselves, "What can I do about it?" Orienting our lives toward our higher power is the most effective answer to this question.

In working step two, we realize that we are not alone. We are deeply connected to God through our relationship with Him and through all that God has created. Reconnecting with others, with nature, with our inner self, we realize that we are part and parcel of our higher power.

In Worksheet 7.2 list specific examples of insanity in your life during your active addiction.

Our Higher Power

A power greater than ourselves is any power that helps us recover from addiction. This power understands our addiction and can help us on the road to recovery. This higher power does not necessarily have to be called God. Our higher power can be personal, such as an intimate relationship with God, or it can be impersonal, such as the experience of pure energy, power, and intelligence. Understandings and experiences of God and a higher power are as many as there are

WORKSHEET 7.2. Working Step Two: Insanity

List specific examples of insanity in your life during your active addiction.

people on this planet, and as variegated and multifaceted. It is not necessary to know the exact nature of a higher power.

The Twelve Steps do not demand anything of us. Rather, they offer suggestions. In AA we are given the freedom to believe, to doubt, and/or to challenge. In step two we are asked to keep an open mind and consider the belief that there is a power greater than ourselves. Through working this step we become open to the infinite possibilities in life outside the bondage of addiction.

In Worksheet 7.3 describe your higher power and your ideas and beliefs about this higher power.

Step Three

In working step three we gain a greater understanding of God, the spiritual foundation of recovery, and the elements and dimensions of spirituality itself.

Step Three reads, "Made a decision to turn our will and our lives over to the care of God as we understood him." This decision is made "just for today." This turning over comes in twenty-four-hour chunks. We turn our will—that is, our thoughts, beliefs, and behaviors—over to the care of God. Our lives involve our actions and behaviors, and it is in step three that we allow God to infuse himself into our lives and we surrender. In effect, we become a prayer to God. We are no longer alone. We no longer lead a life based on sheer will.

This may be difficult for us. It hard to get out of the driver's seat, particularly for executives and professionals. We are no longer running the show, and that can be frightening for us. In step three, we realize that we need God and a higher power in our lives—a belief that it is difficult for many to acknowledge.

It is important to understand that with step three we make a decision to turn over our will and lives. The step does not demand that we act in haste; this step takes time, and it is a process. It would be unrealistic to contemplate or expect an immediate drastic change in our lives. Aligning our wills and our lives with a higher power is a delicate, subtle, daily process. It has no time limit, but it does call for a decision, and that decision is made in step three.

A feeling of relief and a diminished sense of fear often accompany step three. We are deciding to reconnect our lives with the infinite

WORKSHEET 7.3. Working Step Two: Your Higher Power

Name your higher power, and describe your ideas and beliefs about it.

power that underlies and informs all of life. We know that AA is a program of action and calls us to be honest. It requires us to take a serious look at our past thinking, attitudes, and behaviors and to make a concerted effort to change them in the service of our recovery. In working this step, as with all the steps, we do not expect perfection. We look for progress on a daily basis. We make a wholehearted effort to change. The only prerequisite for this program is a sincere desire to stop drinking or drugging.

Step three is about spirituality. The disease of addiction cuts us off from our sense of spirituality. It alienates us from ourselves, others, and God or our higher power. Our spirituality in recovery reunites us with ourselves, others, and God. Worksheet 7.4 asks you consider your experiences of God or a higher power.

PSYCHOLOGICAL DEFENSES AND CHEMICAL DEPENDENCY

Identifying, Understanding, and Reducing Denial

Denial is the most common and the most virulent psychological defense that active addicts use to keep the disease of chemical dependency in place. Denial is a form of lying to ourselves, a fantasy, and an escape from reality. Denial distorts our reality, makes us think and feel that we are in control of alcohol and drugs and that we are managing our lives adequately. When we are in denial, our disease takes on a life of its own, and to stay alive it creates its own story to tell us. It tells us that we are fine, that we do not have a disease, and it fuels continued use of alcohol and drugs. To recover we need to know how our disease betrays us. Recovery requires that we no longer need or want to lie to ourselves. In recovery we allow ourselves to experience the truth, and the truth, as the saying goes, sets us free and heals us.

Denial is a protective device, a defense. Denial is created by the mind to stop us from feeling pain and discomfort and the uncomfortable truths about our powerlessness over alcohol and drugs and the consequences of addiction. With denial we insulate ourselves and continue to believe everything is fine, and our disease stays alive and well.

WORKSHEET 7.4. Working Step Three: Experiences with a Higher Power

In the space below list any experiences you have had with a higher power. Have you ever felt "unseen hands" guiding you or helping you in your life? Have you ever had the experience of letting go of control and sensing a kind of automatic flow in your life, sometimes called "the zone"? Include any positive experiences associated with the experience of a higher power in your recovery.

Denial can be conscious or unconscious. It has eight forms:

1. *Simple Denial.* This is an absolutely flat refusal even to contemplate or consider the truth.
2. *Minimizing.* In this variant of denial, we water down and lessen the effects of chemical dependency. We might say to ourselves, "Yes I do drugs, but I don't do them that often, and I don't drink that much. It really isn't that bad."
3. *Rationalizing.* With this form of denial we make excuses about our alcohol and drug use. We tell ourselves that we need to drink to calm down, or to kill pain, or to help us fall asleep.
4. *Blaming.* In this form of denial, the responsibility for our alcohol and drug use lies outside us—certainly not with us! We may say things to ourselves such as "You'd drink too if your job was as bad as mine," or "Anybody with a marriage like mine would drink," or "My life is depressing; anybody would drink if they had my life."
5. *Bargaining.* In this form of denial, we cut a deal. We put conditions on ceasing our alcohol or drug use. For example, we might say, "I'll stop using drugs when my life becomes less stressful."
6. *Intellectualizing.* In this form of denial we use our intellect and reasoning to come up with an excuse to continue to use alcohol and drugs. We may, for example, blame our alcohol use on bad genes. We may see our alcohol or drug use as a psychological mechanism to deal with the pain of abuse or feelings of inadequacy.
7. *Passivity.* In this form of denial we fall into inaction and we develop a victim mentality. We tell ourselves that we tried to quit many times but that we are just not strong enough to do it. We may feel that we are a failure and develop a "what's the use" mentality.
8. *Hostility.* In this form of denial we may threaten others so that they will not challenge us about our alcohol and drug use. We may, for example, tell our spouse that we will leave if he or she keeps harping on at us about our drinking.

In Worksheet 7.5 write down examples of the various forms of denial that you utilized in your active addiction.

WORKSHEET 7.5. Identifying Denial

In the space below, list examples of the various forms of denial that you utilized in your active addiction. Identify your most frequent form of denial.

Understanding, Assessing, and Managing Anger in Recovery

Most alcoholics and addicts harbor anger, even rage. Many alcoholics grew up in alcoholic families where anger was expressed frequently or suppressed and poorly managed. Alcoholics and addicts have many losses in their background and often feel cheated and neglected. The more losses we incur during active addiction, the angrier we are likely to feel. Alcohol and drugs inflame anger and aggressive acting-out. The surfacing of anger is common in early recovery as the addict or alcoholic begins to deal with the losses, hurts, grief, and frustrations that often are associated with the feeling and expression of anger. Everybody has anger, and everybody has to learn to deal with it adaptively. It is important to understand that anger is a feeling, and as a feeling it is neither good nor bad. It is unwise to make value judgments about anger; anger simply is. Anger is often described as a composite emotion. It may be the blending of many emotions, such as frustration, anxiety, envy, hate, jealousy, hurt, grief, and resentfulness. For many of us, particularly men, anger is an easy emotion to express. Anger expression tends to be more difficult for women. Anger is often associated with hurt. In fact, when we experience anger we almost always have been hurt in some way, but we may cover that hurt up with the expression of anger. It is often difficult to manage anger because many of us feel justified about being angry, especially if we were wronged by others or have lost something dear to us. We may feel that we have earned the right to be angry. Sometimes feeling and expressing anger is entirely appropriate and adaptive. However, during addiction, anger is mismanaged. It is distorted by alcohol and drug use and can lead to self-destructive behavior and hurting others. It can destroy any sense of well-being, serenity, and happiness. Anger often has very negative consequences. During addiction we may sever our relationship with a friend, leave our spouse, or quit a job due to pathological anger.

It is important to identify and deal with anger. Psychologists believe that those who repress anger turn it inward and that this can contribute to depression and other emotional problems. Repressed anger can lead to chronic tension, insomnia, chain-smoking, and passive-aggressive behavior to others, such as being continually late and procrastinating. Some of us have a fear of expressing anger and losing control. We need to deal with this fear and learn how to express anger in healthy ways with the help of a therapist. As addiction progresses, we may become angrier and angrier with ourselves, others, and God. We may be angry with ourselves simply because we are alcoholics or addicts. In Worksheet 7.6 list the consequences of anger during your active addiction.

Remember we have to take responsibility for our anger. We have to identify and accept it. If we have trouble identifying and expressing anger, we need to get help in dealing with anger in a healthful way. If we have trouble controlling our anger we need to seek therapy in an effort to gain control. Other people or things do not "make" us angry. We need to deal with the pain and hurt that may be behind anger. We need to see it as our own personal response to situations and learn to correct the response.

Assessing, Understanding, and Managing Dysfunctional Thoughts and Beliefs in Recovery

The thinking process and the beliefs that we harbor can have a dramatic effect on sustaining addictive behaviors. Likewise, our thoughts and our beliefs can contribute to an addictive disease. Addicts have a number of dysfunctional beliefs with regard to alcohol and drug use:

- Alcohol/drugs will transform my personal experiences in a positive way.
- Alcohol/drugs will enhance my physical and sexual pleasure.
- Alcohol/drugs will make me more socially attractive.
- Alcohol/drugs will make me feel less tense, anxious, or depressed.

In general, addicts believe that drugs and alcohol are essential to maintain adequate functioning in life. The following are additional dysfunctional beliefs about alcohol and drug use:

- Life is boring without drug use.
- My life will not get any better even if I stop using drugs.
- I cannot relax without drugs.
- My life is no fun unless I drink or do drugs.
- Drug use makes me more creative.

WORKSHEET 7.6. Identifying the Consequences of Anger

In the space below, write down examples of the consequences of anger during your active addiction.

Do you agree with any of these beliefs? Complete Worksheet 7.7 to address this matter.

Getting sober involves identifying, challenging, and supplanting the useless dysfunctional ideas, beliefs, and attitudes we have about the role of alcohol and drugs in our lives. During addiction we developed addictive thinking. The effects of alcohol and drugs and the pathological defenses associated with addiction distorted our thoughts. We must realize that our thoughts and beliefs and attitudes are up for debate. They are not truisms. They are merely self-derived interpretations about what is going on with us. We need to purify and straighten out our thinking.

Understanding and Addressing Grief and Loss in Recovery

During addiction, loss and grief are our constant companions. We address loss and grief for the first time in working the first step and realize that we have lost power over alcohol and drug use. We realize alcohol or drug use has destroyed many aspects of our lives, damaged our feelings and our bodies, and hurt others. In working this step we take an inventory of all the things that we have lost because of addiction: relationships, money, a job, education, love, or well-being.

Grief is a normal reaction to and process associated with, loss. Grief is painful. Psychologists say that grief comes in stages. In the first stage, we deny it. We tell ourselves that this cannot be true. As the reality of the loss becomes apparent, we experience a stage of anger. Why has this happened to me? This is not fair. In the third stage, we move past denial, but we may minimize the effects or impact that a particular loss has had in our lives. We may resist making the necessary changes in our life to deal with the loss. Stage four is depression. We feel sorrow and pain, loneliness, and despair. In the final stage of this model we move into deeper levels of the grieving process. We accept our losses and mourn them and we begin to go on with our lives.

We may cycle in and out of these stages many times in recovery as we deal with the losses and confront the grief that our addiction has caused in our lives. In Worksheet 7.8 list the losses that you incurred directly due to your addiction and describe your experience of grief associated with each of these losses.

WORKSHEET 7.7. Identifying Dysfunctional Thoughts

Do you agree with any of the common dysfunctional beliefs about addiction? List them in the space below. After each belief you agree with, list both the advantages and disadvantages of agreeing with this belief. In addition, write down what you would tell a friend or relative who harbored this particular belief about alcohol and drug use.

Belief:

Advantages:

Disadvantages:

What would you tell a friend who had this belief?

Belief:

Advantages:

Disadvantages:

What would you tell a friend who had this belief?

WORKSHEET 7.8. Identifying Losses and Grief

In the space below list the losses that you incurred directly due to your addiction. Describe your experience of grief associated with each of these losses.

In recovery we attend to the suffering that comes from our losses and we utilize it for continued growth. This is known as *posttraumatic growth*. Through the suffering of addiction we become more understanding and compassionate with respect to others. We can begin to appreciate life more and to set appropriate priorities. Our suffering may provide clarity to us about what is important in our lives. We derive strength and renewal from that which does not defeat us. We find more purpose and meaning in life due to our suffering.

FAMILY DYSFUNCTION AND ITS IMPACT ON EMOTIONAL HEALTH AND RECOVERY

Dysfunctional Families

As addicts, many of us came from dysfunctional families. Studies show that American families have some of the highest rates of addiction, as well as mental illness, violence, and suicide. We can be liberated from family dysfunction as we begin to identify and understand the problems in our own family of origin that make us unhealthy and dysfunctional.

A dysfunctional family can be defined as a family where one or more of the individuals do not get their needs met. Family members, children in particular, need unconditional love, acceptance, trust, respect, and recognition. They need to be listened to, they need to be validated, they need to be touched, and they need to feel safe. Family is the social and emotional environment in which we learn to become persons. How we feel about ourselves, how we relate to other people, and our values, our hopes, our aspirations, our priorities, and our goals are shaped by our family experience.

Families, similar to any group, develop rules. These rules are often hidden and silent and they are rarely overtly expressed, but everyone in the family knows them. Some family rules are functional. For example, "Everyone in this family is loved and valued and their input is recognized," "Anyone in this family can talk to another family member about conflict," and "Family members support and encourage each other." However, dysfunctional, addictive families develop unhealthy rules, for example, "In this family, we keep our feelings to ourselves," "Open expression of positive feelings is to be discouraged and criticized if it happens," "Individual privacy does not exist," "Never do anything to make the family look bad," and "Put up or shut up."

In Worksheet 7.9 consider these ideas in the context of your own family.

Dysfunctional families give conditional love. Dysfunctional family members get the message that they are loved if they do something good for the family or if they achieve or if they do not break the unexpressed family rules. Dysfunctional families have many secrets. Addiction can be one of them. Dysfunctional families either lack boundaries or have unusually rigid boundaries. Often dysfunctional families are physically and verbally violent. They use blame and guilt to control family members. Feelings are generally suppressed or censored. Dysfunctional families harbor a great deal of anger, shame, fear, and unhappiness.

As you recover from an addiction it is important to confront the pain you experienced in your family of origin. This is part of breaking through denial and acknowledging problems as they are. Nobody has a perfect childhood. In recovery it is important to learn to identify and tolerate the emotional pain often connected with growing up in a dysfunctional family.

Family Roles

If you grew up in a dysfunctional alcoholic household, chances are you developed one or more roles to cope with the pain of addiction. The family hero copes with pain by achieving through academic, athletic, or financial pursuits. The lost child in the family emotionally withdraws into an inner world to try to escape pain. The family mascot deflects the family's attention away from addiction and engages in humorous activities. Mascots often develop an inordinate need for attention, recognition, and validation. The family scapegoat bears the brunt of the family's anger and other negative emotions that are not directed toward the alcoholic family member. The scapegoat feels unfairly treated because the family cannot directly confront the alcoholic family member, particularly a parent. Instead, the family members take out their frustrations on a less powerful family mem-

WORKSHEET 7.9. Your Family

In the following space, describe your family of origin and any chemically dependent members. Were family members free to express their feelings, both positive and negative? Did your family have family activities. Describe any deep family secrets? What was the atmosphere around the dinner table at home? List any silent, unexpressed family rules you can think of.

ber, the scapegoat. Caretakers use all their energy in taking care of the needs of others—employees, spouse, children, friends, and other family members—at their own expense. They give and give and give until it hurts. They do not take care of themselves. They become self-sacrificing, unhappy, and often depressed. The enabler becomes involved with others who have dysfunctional behaviors, including addiction, and continues the pattern of enabling and ignoring the problems that occured during childhood. Rescuers are attracted to dysfunctional individuals and harbor the inner conviction that they can save such persons from their problems. These roles are often played out in romantic relationships, in friendships, and in the work-place.

In Worksheet 7.10 write down the roles you assumed in your family and their impact on your current behavior.

UNDERSTANDING AND ADDRESSING THE PROCESS OF RELAPSE

Even when we gain some measure of sobriety and serenity, the possibility for internal or external forces to reactivate the disease of addiction and dismantle a recovery program always exists. This can lead to a lapse or a relapse. A lapse is a slip and is defined as the initial use of alcohol or drugs after the patient has made a commitment to abstain. A relapse is a full-blown return to the maladaptive behaviors, feelings, and thoughts originally seen within active addiction. A relapse or lapse usually happens when an individual is confronted with a high-risk situation that he or she has no plans, skills, or resources to deal with. The high-risk situation can be internal or external. One example of an external threat is conflict in a relationship. An internal threat could be depression, anxiety, or another troubling emotion. The high-risk situation can activate basic drug- and alcohol-related beliefs, thoughts, and assumptions, and these can lead to active cravings and urges to use drugs. If you do not have the skills to cope with a high-risk situation, then relapse is likely. Most relapses occur by around the sixth month mark in recovery. The best way to deal with a relapse is proactively. You need to recognize the warning signs of relapse, honestly assess them, and institute a recovery plan to deal with them.

WORKSHEET 7.10. Your Family Roles

In the following space, describe the roles you assumed in your family and their impact on your current behavior.

Some high-risk situations for relapse are:

- The loss of a relationship, job, or money
- Overwhelming feelings of sadness, grief, anxiety, or other negative emotions
- Feeling overly confident in recovery
- Feeling bored or listless in recovery
- Feeling the demands and pressures of family and work life
- Periods of intense conflict at home or at work
- Feeling exhausted
- Feeling lonely and unloved

Among the warning signs of a relapse are the feeling of being stressed out; the emergence of other compulsive behaviors, such as gambling, sex, and perfectionism; the emergence of periods of moodiness; a loss of interest in your recovery program; and a loss of structure in your day-to-day life. In addition, feeling out of control, withdrawing from others, and hiding your feelings and problems can lead to drinking or drugging.

In Worksheet 7.11 list any high-risk situations for relapse you have gone through and any psychological, emotional, physical, or social changes you experienced in these high-risk situations.

Coping with Relapses

1. Become aware of what is happening to you. Remove yourself from a high-risk situation so you can take some time to think and plan.
2. Try to keep calm. If you actually pick up a drug or drink, you may feel a tremendous amount of guilt, self-blame, or shock. You may have "a belly full of booze and a head full of AA." Do not become too caught up in these feeling, and do not be judgmental with yourself. Recommit to sobriety. Resist the urge to think, "What's the use? I've blown it already. I might as well keep on using."
3. When things have settled down, take some time to analyze what happened to you. Come up with a plan to deal with such potential high-risk situations in the future. Ask for help. Talk to your Twelve Steps friends. Call your sponsor. Get on the phone. In-

crease your attendance at Twelve Steps meetings. Read "How it Works" in the Big Book. Take care of your physical and emotional needs. Return to therapy.
4. Be gentle with yourself. Do not give yourself a hard time. Just reactivate your recovery program.

ADDICTION EDUCATION: SELECTED LESSONS

The Disease of Addiction

Addiction is a disease. A disease can be defined as a morbid process with characteristic, identifiable symptoms. The cause of a disease may be known or it may be unknown. Addictive diseases are primary chronic, progressive, relapse-prone, potentially fatal brain diseases characterized by tolerance and a physical dependence that manifests behaviorally in craving, drug seeking behavior and compulsive drug use, loss of control, and continued use of drugs and alcohol despite serious negative consequences.

Addiction is a primary disease. It is not secondary to, or caused by, or a symptom of, another condition. Addiction has no cure. Addiction is progressive. Its signs and symptoms become more severe over time if drug and alcohol use continues. Abstinence is required to stop progression of the disease. Even when the disease of addiction is arrested and deactivated, it carries a continual chance of relapse back to the active illness. Addiction is potentially fatal. It can directly or indirectly kill you.

Tolerance, a sign of addiction, is the result of the body and the brain's adaptation to the presence of alcohol and drugs in the system. The chief sign of tolerance is the need for more and more drugs or alcohol to get the same psychoactive effect. Physical dependence is manifested in withdrawal symptoms when alcohol and drug use stop. Withdrawal symptoms can be mild, moderate, or severe and potentially life threatening. The behavioral symptoms of an addictive disease are:

- Craving, including compulsive drug and alcohol use and drug-seeking behavior
- Loss of control over alcohol and drug use
- Continued use of alcohol and drugs despite severe consequences

WORKSHEET 7.11. Relapse

In the space below list your own high-risk situations for relapse and any psychological, emotional, physical, or social changes you experienced in these high-risk situations.

Signs of craving include preoccupation with alcohol and drug use, thoughts about using, inner conflicts and arguments about using, intrusive thoughts about using, daydreams about using, the experience of withdrawal-like symptoms, and planning to use drugs and alcohol secretly.

Loss of control is the hallmark of an addictive disease. As addiction progresses, an addict may try desperately to limit alcohol or drug use but will fail more often than not. As addiction progresses, the addict is inclined to spend more and more time using alcohol and drugs and being involved in alcohol- and drug-related activities. Attempts to set limits on time, amount, and frequency of use will fail.

Addicts and alcoholics will continue to use drugs despite severe consequences, including job loss, financial ruin, poor health, destruction of family, destruction of friendships and other relationships, and extreme psychological and physical discomfort.

The American Medical Association, the World Health Organization, and the National Institute of Drug Abuse all view addiction as a disease. Addiction is considered a biopsychosocial illness that is genetically based and affected in its manifestation by environmental factors such as family-of-origin experience, family attitudes toward drug and alcohol use, psychosocial stressors, access to drugs, and cultural, ethnic, and racial factors.

Drugs of abuse directly affect the neurotransmitters in the brain, including dopamine, the neurochemical responsible for experiences of pleasure and reward. As drug and alcohol use continue, the brain and neurophysiology are altered by the continual presence of alcohol and drugs in the system. Evidence continues to mount for the genetic basis for addiction and the differences in functioning between an addictive brain and a normal brain.

Establishing Lifestyle Balance: Physical Health in Recovery

When we get sober, physical health often improves dramatically. Unfortunately, many recovering individuals develop habits that undermine the benefits of abstinence. These include poor diet, excessive use of cigarettes and caffeine, and a lack of regular exercise. Eliminate highly processed food such as cakes, candies, and junk food from your diet. Eat three well-balanced meals a day. When you are ready, you should seriously consider a nicotine cessation program. Keep coffee to a minimum. Exercise does not have to be that big of a deal. A brisk walk every day for a half-hour can achieve this goal.

Psychological Help

Be aware of distorted thinking in recovery. Seek help if you are constantly thinking in a pessimistic way or if you are overly judgmental or overly critical. Distorted, irrational, unhealthy thinking can lead to problems with the management of moods and emotions and subsequent behaviors. In the first year of recovery, distorted, unhealthy thinking that you reduced during your treatment may return. Seek out therapy or self-help books to help you combat irrational, dysfunctional thinking. You may also be prone to moodiness or emotional sensitivity during the first few months of recovery. Learn to anticipate this. Be gentle with yourself. Talk to others. Seek professional help if it is necessary. You also have to be aware of maintaining a balance in your behavior. Say the Serenity Prayer often and invite God into your daily life. In family and intimate relationships, it is important to communicate openly and honestly and to resist any impulse to withdraw. Conflict is inevitable; do not ignore it. You must deal with it assertively and skillfully. Do not let resentments build up from conflict in relationships. Be aware of any imbalance in your lifestyle, particularly overwork. Do not let yourself get too tired or stressed. Attend to your spiritual health, meditate, go to church or temple, and make sure you have a lot of sober fun. It is paramount to experience and express gratitude for your recovery as often as you can.

Addressing Guilt and Shame

Guilt involves feeling responsible for an offense or a wrongdoing. It also involves remorseful awareness or having done something wrong or having failed to do something required or expected. Guilt comes from within us and derives from our sense of values of what is right and wrong. Guilt occurs following conflict or when we are placed in a dilemma between what is right or wrong and the thoughts and behaviors that we are contemplating. Extreme guilt can result from an overly punitive conscience. Normal guilt is a healthy way of promoting our capacity to make choices and reinforce those values we believe in. It can be an internally derived negative consequence when we act against our own values. Constructive guilt is a healthy sign that we have a conscience and that we know the difference between right and wrong. When guilt is too intense, it can become destructive. We may become convinced that we are totally horrible, bad people and we can give up hope for any positive change. Working the steps and getting appropriate therapy, combined with spiritual practices, can reduce pathological guilt.

Shame is a painful feeling brought on by a sense of guilt, embarrassment, unworthiness, or disgrace. Shame is a reaction to letting others down. It almost always occurs in a social context. Healthy shame can help us live balanced lives in accord with acceptable behavior. Pathological shame can immobilize us and can take away hope.

Addicts often come from households that use shame and guilt to control behavior. It is important to realize that addiction blocks us from accurate and valid value judgments, choices, and behaviors. We need to be alert to the development of unhealthy levels of shame and guilt and take the necessary action to bring our psychology back into balance. We do not have to take responsibility for being an addict, but we do have to take responsibility for our recovery. We must learn to be accepting of our faults, our imperfections, and ourselves. We must see the divine in all of us, that we were made in the image and likeness of God.

Ten Tasks for Recovery

Task 1

Stop using. Drugs alter the way we think, feel, and act. When we stop alcohol and drugs we allow the brain and body to cleanse themselves of the neurotoxic effects. We break the cycle of intoxication, withdrawal, and repeat drug use. During addiction we may have tried several ways to deal with our drug use, such as cutting back on consumption or switching to a "lesser" drug (e.g. substituting marijuana for cocaine). We also may have given up some drugs but not others. We need extended abstinence to lay the foundation for sobriety.

Task 2

Learn about your disease. Read all you can about addiction and become an expert on addictive diseases. Talk to your sponsor, your counselor, and your doctor. Go on the Internet and read all you can about the physiological, psychological, social, and spiritual effects of addiction.

Task 3

Use your information to self-diagnose and self-assess. Apply all that you have learned about addiction through self-assessment. Identify your symptoms of addiction. It does not matter how many other people diagnose you as an addict; you must self-diagnose and believe it. Self-diagnosis is an important task because it motivates recovery itself. To promote the task of self-diagnosis, learn to "identify not compare." Look for the similarities between yourself and other addicts, but do not use the differences as a basis for trying to convince yourself that you are not chemically dependent. Realize that you may not have all of the signs and symptoms of an addictive disease. Be aware of the defense mechanisms that block self-diagnosis, such as denial, rationalization, externalization, minimizing, and projection. Addicts are well defended. Do everything you can to stop your defense mechanisms from blocking your ability to see the truth.

Task 4

Reduce your frame of reference to a single day. Expect to go through many emotional changes during recovery. Each day your nervous system is making adjustments to deal with abstinence. You may become stress sensitive. You may become moody. Your nerves may feel raw. Realize that this is normal in recovery. Keep your focus on managing your feelings for a single twenty-four-hour period. Do not expect good health to come instantly. Be gentle with yourself. Forgive yourself if you explode in a fit of anger. Do not place too many unrealistic expectations upon yourself. Do not stress yourself out. You are recuperating and healing. Get lots of rest. Be your own best friend. Resist the urge to project into the future and to mull over the past. Stay in the present. Deal with what is right in front of you.

There will be a time and a place to heal past wounds and plan future activities; however, in early recovery, the focus should stay on each twenty-four-hour period.

Task 5

Rearrange your activities to support recovery. Recovery is largely a matter of priorities. It should always be at the top of your list. If you let your abstinence drop from its place of prime importance, you may lose your program of recovery. Stay away from the people, places, and things of your addiction. Do what you can to make your job and hobbies and social activities more recovery friendly.

Task 6

Make abstinence unconditional. Although it is tough to remain clean in the face of problems, it is exactly what you have to do. Do not make your sobriety dependent on circumstances or conditions. Do not say to yourself, "I'll stay away from drugs as long as things don't get too stressful," for example. Do not let anything in your life become more important than your recovery, because without your recovery you may not have a life! If you stay sober your chances of solving the problems that confront you are much greater than if you use.

Task 7

Inform others of your recovery plan. Build a support system around you. Socialize with other sober people. Let others know what you need. Help others understand your situation. Let the people who are important in your life know about your recovery plan. Solicit their help when appropriate. Do not hide out in secret in recovery. This does not mean you have to tell everybody you are a recovering addict, but it does mean that you should have a group of people with whom you can be completely honest and open about your disease.

Task 8

Examine the factors that might contribute to relapse in the initial stage of recovery. Both external and internal factors can dismantle your recovery program. External factors could include past occasions in your life when you used, relationships that are characterized by a great deal of conflict, predictable crises in your life, and using friends or drinking buddies. Internal factors include attitudes that can breed discontent, such as feeling that life is not fair because you are addicted, resenting that you are similar to other chemically dependent people, having the feeling that sobriety and abstinence are boring, or feeling burdened by the tasks of recovery and the changes that you have continually to make.

Task 9

Develop a plan to prevent relapse. Work with your sponsor or therapist to address chronic conflicts in your life. Learn ways to view and deal with these conflicts differently. Take a proactive approach to dealing with stresses and crises in your life. Plan your work and work your plan. Stay away from drug-abusing friends and acquaintances. Make new friends and engage in new activities. Resist the urge to believe thoughts and attitudes that are counterproductive in recovery. Just because you think something or feel something does not necessarily make it true.

Task 10

Put recovery plans into action. Plan your work and work your plan. Continue to build your knowledge about addiction in recovery. Continue to be truthful, open, and honest with others. Take a daily inventory of your recovery efforts. Put the principles of AA into action on a daily basis.

Ways to Fail in Recovery

For many reason an addict can refuse to do the things which enable him or her to stay clean and sober. Engaging in counterproductive activities that undermine the positive steps you are taking in recovery can lead to relapse to active addiction. Certain patterns of failure have been identified in patients who do not stay clean and sober. If you recognize any of the following patterns, you will need to take steps to prevent them or deal with them if they become evident.

Pattern 1. No Self-Diagnosis

This is a failure to complete step one. Here you are continuing to doubt the diagnosis of addiction and you believe that you can use successfully at some time in the future.

Pattern 2. Experiments with Controlled Use

Here the addict believes willpower will prevent uncontrolled drug or alcohol use, so it is safe to use again.

Pattern 3. Maintaining a Using Environment

Here the addict may stop using but spends long periods with other people who continue to use drugs and drink. This pattern involves the refusal to give up old places, people, and things associated with active addiction. Remember, if you hang around a barbershop long enough, you are going to get a haircut.

Pattern 4. Stress

With this pattern, problems mount during recovery and become overwhelming. The stress associated with them may lead the addict to believe he or she is justified in using again to deal with stress. Stress does not cause addiction, and it does not have to cause relapse either. Take responsibility for your recovery and engage in stress management techniques.

Pattern 5. Overconfidence

Overconfidence can rear its head as the serious problems associated with active drug use begin to fade from memory. Things start going very well. Addicts can become complacent and even overconfident, feeling that they have licked the problem of addiction once and for all. Once this attitude sets in, the need for a recovery program appears to dissolve.

Pattern 6. Lack of Awareness of Normal Recovery Symptoms

Addicts who lack proper education about addiction and relapse may become overly concerned with symptoms such as sleep disturbance, short-term memory problems, vivid dreams about using, fluctuations in moods and feelings, fatigue, or temporary problems with sexual impotence. These symptoms can be a normal part of recovery. Do not be too upset about them. Do not use because of them. If they persist, go to a doctor and get appropriate help.

Pattern 7. Poor Nutrition

If you do not get proper nutrition and eat regular meals, you are not going to feel well. Do not go for long periods of time without eating, and do not eat too much processed food.

Pattern 8. The Family Feud

Your family still feel the effects of your active addiction. They may have difficulty with the disease concept and think it is just irresponsibility on your part. They are still angry about what you did during your active addiction. They may feel you have to prove your self-worth and win their loyalty and love again. Many family members continue to hold grudges. They may punish you for being an addict and causing family problems. Do what you can to help your family understand the disease process and the process of recovery. Encourage AA attendance. If the family conflict and arguments are severe, seek out family therapy with a knowledgeable addictions therapist.

Slogans to Remember

> Keep it simple.
> Let go and let God.
> Meeting makers make it.
> Easy does it.
> One drink equals insanity.
> Pour me, pour me, and pour me a drink.
> Keep coming back.
> Be gentle with yourself.
> One is too many; a thousand is not enough.
> Remember to remember.
> This too shall pass.
> I can't, God can, I think I'll let him.

Share your pain.
There is a God and you're not it.
Learn to listen and listen to learn.
Recovery is a journey, not a destination.
There is no problem so bad that a drink can't make it worse.
Don't quit five minutes before the miracle happens.
You are not alone.
Remember your last drunk.

Normal Symptoms in the Early Stage of Recovery: Understanding and Dealing with Cravings

"Craving" is a nonspecific term for any form of spontaneous desire to use a drug or drink. Your physiology and past learning combine as your body calls out for its favorite toxins. Three types of cravings can be experienced:

- *Free-floating craving.* This type of craving seems to come out of the blue and may be related to some subtle physiological or psychological cue that is out of awareness.
- *Craving due to emotional excitement.* Cravings can arise when your emotions or moods go to extremes in either a positive or negative direction, for example, elation and depression.
- *Condition craving.* This is set off by an environmental cue—anything from seeing old drug-using buddies to watching a commercial for beer to seeing a documentary on drugs on television.

Cravings vary greatly in their nature and intensity. It is important for you to recognize and deal with cravings. Cravings can lead to euphoric but distorted memories about how wonderful you felt when you were under the influence of alcohol and drugs. They can lead to intense dreams about using. They can take the form of obsessive thoughts that crowd into your mind. They can be associated with actively planning to relapse to active alcohol and drug use. When cravings rise in intensity, they activate addiction-based defenses such as denial, rationalization, and minimization. When you get a craving you can do any number of the following:

- Get involved in vigorous exercise.
- Eat something.

- Talk to someone about the craving.
- Distract yourself with a pleasurable activity.
- Use self-hypnosis relaxation techniques in meditation.
- Remove yourself from the situation that may be cueing the craving.
- Go to an AA or NA meeting.

Most cravings fluctuate and come and go. They are time limited. Allow them to come, peak, and resolve. Refocus your attention on recovery.

Understanding Emotional Augmentation

During active addiction, drugs blunt or flatten emotional responses such as fear, anger, sadness, and grief. During early recovery, these feelings can be experienced in an augmented or magnified fashion. You may experience intense feelings of many different types during early recovery. They may feel as if they are an overreaction to what stimulates them. Recognize and anticipate augmented emotions in early recovery. They are actually a normal part of the healing process. Do not take them too seriously, and refocus on recovery efforts.

Common Psychophysiological Symptoms in Early Recovery

Insomnia

Addicts in early recovery regularly report insomnia. Do not become alarmed by it. Your body is continuing to rebalance itself, and in time normal sleep will come. Resist the urge to use psychoactive sleep aids. Try a hot bath, a massage, or a relaxation technique to help you fall asleep naturally.

Mood Swings and Depressive Episodes

Mood irregularities such as overexcitement and depression are common in early recovery. From time to time you may experience despair, hopelessness, apathy, emotional flatness indecisiveness, concentration problems, or just feeling out of sorts. Monitor you moods. If feelings of sadness or depression continue for weeks at a time then see your doctor. You may have a coexisting depressive disorder that is not associated with mood irregularities in early recovery.

Anxiety

Anxiety is a feeling of dread, as though something awful is about to happen. Anxiety has both mental and physical symptoms. Mental symptoms include wary, catastrophic thinking and awfulizing, and physical symptoms include pounding heart, feeling light headed, difficulty with breathing, and feeling as if you are going to faint. Anxiety episodes are usually relatively short lived, passing in a matter of minutes. Over time in recovery they decrease in severity, frequency, and duration. You may experience anxiety when you confront situations in recovery that you normally dealt with by using alcohol or drugs. Use meditation, relaxation, and spirituality to deal with anxiety. However, if anxiety persists or seems to get worse, consult your family doctor.

Food Cravings

Newly recovering addicts often report all sorts of weird food cravings—mostly for sugary snacks. It is recommended that you restrict your sugar intake, limit caffeinated beverages, exercise regularly, and take vitamin supplements.

Flashback Experiences

Sometimes the symptoms of drug toxicity recur from time to time in abstinence. This is particularly true for those who used hallucinogenic drugs. Flashbacks are generally harmless; do not make too much out of them. However, if they persist or cause a great deal of anxiety, see a physician.

Sexual Dysfunction

During addiction addicts regularly experience problems such as occasional impotence, difficulty achieving orgasm, diminished sex drive, or overly sexual behavior. During early recovery your mind and body are undergoing profound normalization, and this also extends to your sexual functioning. Again, do not be too concerned about fluctuations in your sexual drive or experiences. Again, if they persist see a doctor.

Forgetfulness

Serious prolonged use of alcohol and other drugs can result in ongoing memory problems. Most memory problems, however, clear up within the first year of abstinence.

Aches, Pains, and Cramping

These symptoms are reported frequently in early recovery, especially in addicts who have old injuries that have been covered up by alcohol and drug use. We recommend relaxing baths, hydrotherapy, massage, self-hypnosis, and meditation as aids for increasing comfort. If you are in chronic pain, a number of non-addictive pain medications can be prescribed by your physician.

Colds and Infections

Patients regularly report an increase in colds and respiratory infections in early recovery. Remember to take care of yourself, engage in preventive medicine, and get lots of rest.

Weight Loss/Weight Gain

Many addicts, particularly alcoholics and stimulant-dependent individuals, experience significant weight gain in recovery. During addiction you may not have eaten properly. During active addiction, particularly alcoholism, the body's ability to absorb nutrients can be compromised. During early recovery the body is trying to balance itself. The biggest culprit in weight gain is almost always a bad diet. Eat nutritious foods. Avoid crash or fad diets.

Post–Acute Withdrawal

After the initial withdrawal syndrome is over, you feel a lot better, probably for a few weeks. As your recovery continues, however, post–acute withdrawal symptoms may become manifest. These are due to the neurotoxic effects associated with active addiction. Post–acute withdrawal symptoms are a group of symptoms that occur after acute withdrawal has run its course. Post–acute withdrawal is defined as a psychosocial syndrome that results from a combination of damage to the nervous system caused by drug and alcohol use and the psychosocial stress of coping with life without chemicals. The severity of post–acute withdrawal depends on the severity of the neurophysiological damage due to addiction and the amount of psychosocial stress you experience in recovery. Damage due to active addiction is usually reversible with proper treatment and abstinence. Post–acute withdrawal symptoms can last from six to twenty-four months into abstinence; however, they usually peak within the first three to six months. Post–acute withdrawal symptoms vary in severity, frequency, and duration. Various patterns in the resolution of these symptoms are seen. Symptoms generally improve the longer a person stays sober. However, some individuals experience an increase in the intensity of post–acute withdrawal the longer sobriety lasts. Sometimes individuals experience a stable post–acute withdrawal picture—symptoms neither get worse nor resolve. Sometimes the symptoms are intermittent: symptoms come and go and fluctuate over time.

Symptoms of post–acute withdrawal include the following:

- *An inability to think clearly.* This includes difficulties in concentrating, difficulties in solving complex or abstract problems, and rigid or repetitive thinking.
- *Memory problems.* This includes short-term memory and long-term memory. Memory problems can make it difficult to learn new skills and acquire new information.
- *Emotional overreaction or numbness.* In early recovery, individuals often experience intense emotional reactions such as anger, fear, and anxiety. Some individuals experience the opposite. They feel a flattening, blunting, or numbing of emotions and experience a form of emotional shutdown, especially in the face of stress. Mood swings are also a part of the syndrome.
- *Sleep problems.* These include unusual or disturbing dreams, difficulty falling or staying asleep, sleeping for long periods, and sleeping during the day.

- *Physical coordination problems.* These include dizziness, balance problems, problems with eye–hand coordination, and feeling clumsy, along with slower reflexes.
- *Difficulty managing stress.* Included here are the problems of a diminished awareness of stress and difficulty recognizing the signs of stress, a difficult time relaxing, always feeling overstressed, and fearing that stress will lead you to fall apart physically or mentally.
- *Difficulty staying in touch with reality.* This includes periods of confusion, alienation, and feeling disconnected from your body, your environment, and others.

Managing Post–Acute Withdrawal Symptoms

Discuss your post–acute withdrawal symptoms in counseling and with others in recovery. Sharing brings some relief. Read about post–acute withdrawal and find out how others in recovery have dealt with this problem. Develop different methods of coping with the psychosocial stress of recovery; for example, learn self-hypnosis, learn to meditate properly, engage in stress reduction techniques, work out regularly, get a regular massage, investigate complementary and alternative medicine, take good care of yourself, eliminate stress when you can and manage it when it occurs, and make sure you have balanced nutrition and plenty of time for relaxation and pleasure.

Comparing In/Comparing Out: Patterns of Addictive Use

As you work the first step and self-diagnose you may find evidence that leads you to believe you are not an addict. You may listen to other addicts stories and say to yourself, "At least that hasn't happened to me." This process is called *comparing out*. It is a part of the addictive process. It is distorted thinking that leads an addict to believe he or she is not really an addict. The comparing-out process is based on the erroneous assumption that to qualify as an addict you have to have all the symptoms of a disease. This is not true. As you assess your addiction, even if it has not become that bad yet, you can be guaranteed that if you continue it will get worse. The way to deal with comparing out and to correct self-delusion is called *comparing in.* Here you focus on the symptoms that you do have, not the ones that you do not have. This can lead to an attitude change toward the treatment and toward recovery. You come to believe that you have the disease, that it is treatable, that you want a better life, and that you are willing to do the necessary work to stay sober. The key to this conversion is education. One of the addict's first tasks is to learn something about how addicts actually use alcohol and drugs. You can then use this information for self-diagnosis.

Drug and Alcohol Use Patterns

Maintenance

In this pattern of use, addicts maintain a "comfortable" blood level of a drug in their system. This is usually somewhere between intoxication and withdrawal. The area between the boundaries of intoxication and withdrawal is called the *comfort zone.* All long-term drug addicts learn to take just enough drugs to maintain the comfort zone style of functioning. This is particularly true of sedative hypnotic drugs such as alcohol, tranquilizers, and narcotics. Many addicts sustain this maintenance pattern for decades before they experience the loss of control that is the hallmark of addiction. Going through life in the comfort zone makes them feel that they are stable. However, as soon as they move into abstinence, extreme discomfort rears its head and the damage associated with lengthy drug use becomes apparent. As addiction progresses, many addicts move from a maintenance using pattern to one of loss of control.

Loss of Control

In this pattern of drug use the addict progressively loses control over use along four lines: the amount used, the time when use occurs, the place where using occurs, and the length of the using episode. The speed of progression of this pattern is probably genetically mediated. Over time, as addiction progresses, loss of control becomes more frequent and of longer duration. In between bouts of loss of control addicts in this pattern of drug use may have periods when they use "normally." This represents a fallback into an active maintenance pattern.

Over time, periods of maintenance become shorter and shorter and periods of loss of control get longer and longer.

Abstinence/Binge

Addicts who show this pattern have a succession of dry and bingeing periods. Over time the dry periods tend to get shorter and shorter and the binges will get longer and more frequent. The key to self-diagnosis is to look at patterns of drug use over time. During periods of bingeing, loss of control associated with an active addictive disease becomes very obvious.

Basics of Recovery

It is important to keep recovery simple by focusing on the basics:

1. Do not pick up a pill, fix a drink, smoke a pipe, etc.
2. Stay away from the people, places, and things of your addiction.
3. Become and stay honest. Be aware of self-deception. Continually focus on the acceptance of your disease. Do not harbor secrets.
4. Help another addicted person. Share your knowledge and experience with him or her. Go to meetings. Get involved in sponsorship. Do Twelve Steps calls.
5. Get a sponsor and follow his or her directions.
6. Go to meetings.
7. Work the steps.
8. Turn it over to a higher power.

CONCLUSION

Periodically reviewing the information in this lesson can help strengthen and solidify the foundation of your recovery program. The lesson contains essential information and ideas for promoting sobriety. Return to it often in the first year of recovery to anchor your understanding of the disease of addiction and of areas of your functioning you should be addressing on a regular basis.

Appendix

The O'Connell Dysfunctional
Attitude Survey (ODAS)

INTRODUCTION

This is a survey of beliefs, attitudes, and assumptions you may
have about yourself, others, and life in general. I developed this instrument based on my six years of experience treating addicted executives, professionals, and other patients. Our attitudes and beliefs
about ourselves are based to a large extent on core values we develop
during our childhood and adolescent years. Many of them come from
our family experience. They reflect what we learn to survive emotionally in our family and later at school, in the work environment,
and in the world in general. Some of the attitudes and beliefs that we
learn are adaptive and help us cope with problems in life. Others are
dysfunctional or maladaptive and work against us, depriving us of
happiness, well-being, and self-esteem. Since our feelings and our
psychological outlook in life are intimately bound up with our core
values, beliefs, and attitudes, it can be useful to identify and assess
them. Through this process we can identify our strengths and embrace our positive qualities. This can lead to greater feelings of self-
worth. Identifying and assessing maladaptived ysfunctional attitudes
and beliefs can help us pinpoint our emotional liabilities and character defects so that we can begin to address them and reduce or eliminate them, if we can, in our recovery program.

In completing this survey you will express your level of agreement or disagreement with a wide variety of statements. In taking the test, be as honest as you can. In assessing whether you agree with a statement and how much you agree with it, look at the bigger picture of your life not just at how things have been going in your recent recovery program. If you have been behaving, feeling, or thinking as if you agree or disagree with any particular statement, then your answer should reflect that level of agreement. Do not base your answers in this test on how you would like to think or feel or how you should think or feel. Be honest, be open, and be objective.

This survey attempts to identify attitudes, beliefs, and thoughts that can be problematic for you in recovery. However, it is not a comprehensive psychological test or personality inventory. It focuses on a fairly narrow category and range of attitudes and beliefs often harbored by executives, professionals, and those in leadership positions. It is not a published test and has not been subjected to rigorous statistical analysis. It is simply a survey that I have found useful in helping executive patients in recovery get well.

THE SURVEY

Directions

On the following pages, you will indicate your level of agreement or disagreement with a series of statements. After reading each statement and reflecting, check the appropriate box. After you are done taking the test, read the scoring directions that follow it. You will come up with six scores, which you then enter on the graph that follows the scoring directions. An example of scoring has been provided for you. After you have entered your scores on the graph, turn to the next section, which provides an interpretation of your ODAT scores. These interpretations will help you better understand your personality dynamics relative to the six domains assessed by the survey. Good luck, and have fun.

	Agree Strongly	Agree Slightly	Neutral	Disagree Slightly	Disagree Strongly
I. Validation					
1. In my life, I have had to live up to others' standards and expectations.					
2. Criticism and disapproval from others secretly devastates me.					
3. It has been important for me to impress others with my achievements and credentials.					
4. Without attention and approval from others, I feel low self-esteem.					
5. If I am expected to do something for someone, I should absolutely do it despite any negative consequences for me.					
6. I need other people's approval in order to be happy.					
7. If someone does not like me or disapproves of me, most likely something is wrong with me.					
II. Achievement					
8. Self-worth is really dependent on being outstanding in at least one area of my life.					
9. Other people may not have to have a high level of achievement, but I definitely do.					
10. I am a human "doing" more than a human being.					

	Agree Strongly	Agree Slightly	Neutral	Disagree Slightly	Disagree Strongly
11. Winning is not everything; it is the only thing.					
12. Being productive is the most important thing in life.					
13. If I do not win the activity, competition, or game I am involved in, then inwardly I feel as if I am a failure.					
14. A person has to achieve something great in life if he or she is to be a worthwhile individual.					
III. Affective Control					
15. Showing your true feelings can be dangerous and can have negative consequences.					
16. Experiencing tender feelings such as affection embarrasses me and makes me anxious.					
17. Showing your feelings will make you vulnerable and should generally be avoided.					
18. I know if I let myself really feel all the pain I have had in life, I will completely fall apart.					
19. Controlling the expression of feelings is the mark of a mature person.					
20. I value my intellect and reasoning much more than my emotions and intuition.					

	Agree Strongly	Agree Slightly	Neutral	Disagree Slightly	Disagree Strongly
21. "Don't ever let them see you sweat" is good advice in your business and your private life.					
IV. Perfectionism					
22. I only try a new activity or skill when I know I can expect to excel at it.					
23. I feel that if I make a mistake it means that I am incompetent.					
24. Even after I work hard and achieve something, I never really enjoy my success.					
25. I have to set the highest standards for myself, and if I do not achieve them I am definitely second rate.					
26. I secretly believe that I should be in control all the time, in all situations.					
27. I often feel as if I am a fraud; that is why I have to work so hard and be on top of everything.					
28. I almost always notice what is wrong or negative with myself and others, rather than what is right or positive.					
V. Egocentricity					
29. I absolutely expect to get something if I deserve it.					
30. It is horribly frustrating if you encounter obstacles that block you from what you want to do.					

	Agree Strongly	Agree Slightly	Neutral	Disagree Slightly	Disagree Strongly
31. When something goes wrong at work or at home, I automatically assume it is my responsibility and I am at fault.					
32. When I think of it, I am really to blame for most of the problems that others in my life experience.					
33. Others would describe me as a demanding, uncompromising person.					
34. I deserve special treatment.					
35. If things do not go my way, I get depressed.					
VI. Drivenness					
36. I feel empty if I am not constantly doing something.					
37. Time is definitely running out.					
38. If I am honest, I believe that no matter how much I have, it's never enough.					
39. You have to be obsessed with success if you are going to make it in this life.					
40. I learned early in life that I have to prove myself constantly and achieve—I know no other way.					
41. I live my life by burning the candle at both ends.					
42. I cannot stop pushing myself to do more and more.					

SCORING DIRECTIONS

To score the ODAS, enter your scores into Figure A.1. The test is scored as follows:

Strongly agree = −2
Agree slightly = −1
Neutral = 0
Disagree slightly = +1
Disagree strongly = +2

Go over each of the items in each of the six sections of the test. Enter your scores in the central section and then add them up in the column under "Total Scores." Remember that when you add a negative score to a positive score, you subtract it. Your scores are grouped according to the following six dimensions: validation, achievement, affective control, perfectionism, egocentricity, and drivenness. Each of these dimensions is measured through seven test items.

Figure A.2 shows a sample completed score chart. When you are done scoring the test, enter your score on the graph for each of the six dimensions in Figure A.3. Figure A.4 shows a sample graph for the scores from Figure A.2. Scores from 1 to +14 indicate psychological strengths. Scores from 1 to −14 indicate psychological liabilities or vulnerabilities. When you are done scoring the test and entering your scores on the graph, go to the next section for an interpretation of your ODAT scores.

Value System	Attitudes	Individual Scores							Total Scores
I. Validation	1 to 7								
II. Achievement	8 to 14								
III. Affective Control	15 to 21								
IV. Perfectionism	22 to 28								
V. Egocentricity	29 to 35								
VI. Drivenness	36 to 42								

FIGURE A.1. ODAS scoring chart.

Value System	Attitudes	Individual Scores							Total Scores
I. Validation	1 to 7	+2	+2	+2	0	−2	−1	−1	+2
II. Achievement	8 to 14	0	+1	+1	0	0	−2	−2	−2
III. Affective Control	15 to 21	0	+1	+1	+2	+2	−2	0	+4
IV. Perfectionism	22 to 28	−2	0	−2	+1	+1	+2	0	0
V. Egocentricity	29 to 35	0	−2	−2	−2	+2	+2	0	−2
VI. Drivenness	36 to 42	+2	+1	+1	0	0	0	0	+4

FIGURE A.2. Sample completed ODAS scoring chart.

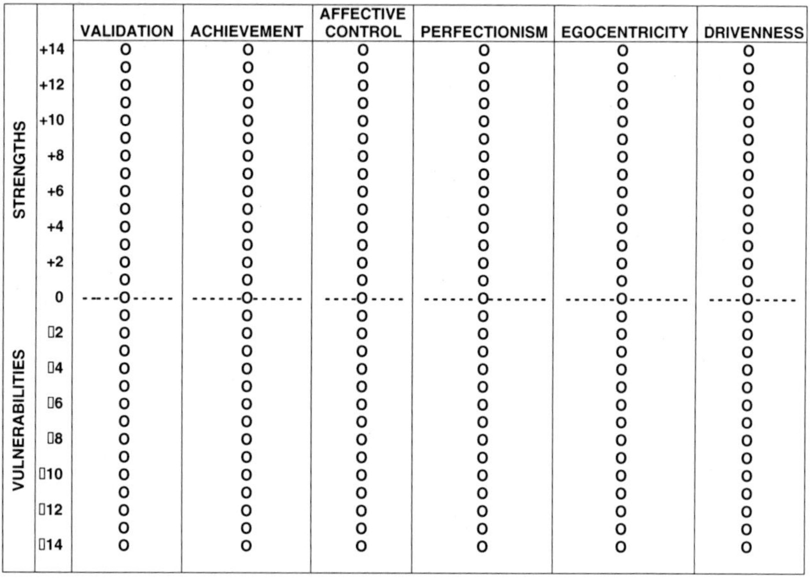

FIGURE A.3. ODAS Scores Graph

INTERPRETATION

Now that you have scored and graphed your test results, read through the interpretation. Remember that the following interpretations are general. They point to or suggest a style of thinking and re-

		VALIDATION	ACHIEVEMENT	AFFECTIVE CONTROL	PERFECTIONISM	EGOCENTRICITY	DRIVENNESS
STRENGTHS	+14	O	O	O	O	O	O
	+12	O	O	O	O	O	O
	+10	O	O	O	O	O	O
	+8	O	O	O	O	O	O
	+6	O	O	O	O	O	O
	+4	O	O	O	O	O	O
	+2	O	O	O	O	O	O
	0	O	O	O	O	O	O
VULNERABILITIES	-2	O	O	O	O	O	O
	-4	O	O	O	O	O	O
	-6	O	O	O	O	O	O
	-8	O	O	O	O	O	O
	-10	O	O	O	O	O	O
	-12	O	O	O	O	O	O
	-14	O	O	O	O	O	O

FIGURE A.4. Sample Completed ODAS Scores Graph

lating you have developed with respect to yourself, others, and life in general. The higher or lower your score, the more or less you manifest certain traits, behaviors, and patterns of thinking and attitudes. Remember that this is not a definitive, comprehensive psychological test. You are a complex individual. A simple attitudinal inventory is not going to capture that complexity. Remember also that nothing in life is permanent. As you read the interpretation of the test results, you may agree or disagree with the material you read and you may feel good or bad about it. Keep in mind that you can change limiting beliefs and attitudes. They are not written in stone. This is the whole point of recovery from addictions. This test will help you become more aware of defects of character and maladaptive thinking patterns so that you can take some action to change them. The test also apprises you of the strengths and assets that will assist you in the recovery process. You can use the results of this inventory to address your concerns in counseling or with your twelve-step sponsor. Remember it is not a diagnostic test and not a substitute for your counselor or therapist's assessment of your strengths and weaknesses.

I. Validation

Negative Score

A negative score on validation indicates that you are much too other-focused—that is, other people's opinions of you matter too much. This places you in a dependent position because you are constantly judging yourself and evaluating yourself according to other people's reactions to you. If their feedback happens to be negative, you take it to be reality and you look down on yourself and can become excessively self-critical. You engage too much in impression management—you are excessively focused on making a good impression on others and hoping for their approval. You are constantly focusing on what you imagine other people think of you. This puts you in a vulnerable position and you can be easily manipulated. Your self-esteem and moods tend to waver depending whether you like the validation you are getting from others. Codependent individuals score low in this dimension. You need constant reassurance and you become overly concerned with your performance at work and at home. You do what is expected of you, not what you really want to do. You have an inordinate need for recognition that leaves your life out of balance.

Positive Score

A positive score indicates that you are a relatively independent, self-directed, self-reliant individual with a healthy sense of self-worth. You tend to enjoy your accomplishments for their own sake and for the sense of joy they give you rather than for their impact on others. Although you may enjoy being admired and praised, admiration and praise are not essential to you. You tend to look inward rather than outward for the sense of who you are.

II. Achievement

Negative Score

A negative score indicates your self-esteem and sense of well-being are intimately tied to your productivity and accomplishments in life. Workaholics score low on this dimension. You set unrealistic expectations for yourself and you push yourself constantly. Inwardly you are constantly comparing yourself with others. A deep sense of inferiority and inadequacy may drive you to overcompensate and overachieve. You are guided by the mistaken belief that if only you achieve some type of external success, then everything one day will be okay and you will feel worthwhile as a person. You overidentify with your job, and your job or profession may become your identity. You may feel uncomfortable with silence and unstructured time. Intimacy may be difficult for you. Just "being," rather than constant doing, is extremely difficult. Your life is out of balance because you overextend yourself and you are involved in too many projects and cannot say no. You may feel a sense of resentment because of this, and you may suffer from periodic exhaustion.

Positive Score

A positive score indicates that you enjoy your achievements and accomplishments for their own sake not as methods to bolster your sense of self-worth and self-esteem. You feel satisfied. You enjoy your work. You enjoy quiet time, unstructured activities, and leisure time. You are able to "turn off" your mental focus on work when you leave the workplace and come home. You feel relaxed. You function in the moment rather than constantly projecting into the future.

III. Affective Control

Negative Score

A negative score indicates that you are uncomfortable with your emotional life. You tend to suppress, repress, or avoid emotions when you can. You are uncomfortable with intimacy and the expression of tender feelings. You equate emotional openness with weakness and vulnerability. You are afraid of losing emotional control if you actually access and express your feelings. The lower the score, the more out of touch with your feelings you are. In fact, you may feel emotionally blunted and flat or experience very little in the way of feelings. You prize self-control. You value rational and logical thinking at the expense of feelings and your intuitive side. You tend to be judgmental and critical of others whom you see as too emotional. As a consequence you may feel lonely, cut off, and separate from others. Your family members may complain that they never know your real feelings. When you do show feelings, they tend all to be negative, such as angry outbursts or feelings of anxiety and depression. You may feel a vague sense of tension. Your favorite character on *Star Trek* is Mr. Spock!

Positive Score

A positive score indicates that you are emotionally free, balanced, spontaneous, and comfortable with the full range of your emotions. You do not overvalue your rational thinking abilities and see them as opposed to your more emotional, intuitive abilities. You feel comfortable with yourself and with others. You are aware of your own feelings, as well as those of others, and you are able to respond appropriately in emotionally charged situations. You have a high capacity for intimacy. You are comfortable in your own skin. You are not rigidly defended against unpleasant feelings or impulses. You are self-accepting and, as a consequence, others accept you and are drawn to you.

IV. Perfectionism

Negative Score

A negative score indicates that you demand perfectionism in yourself, and possibly in others. You have a deep fear of failure, which motivates many of your behaviors. You do not allow yourself to make mistakes, and when you doerr you can become self-punishing and hypercritical of yourself. You look at life as an all-or-nothing proposition. You are either a winner or a loser. Others may describe you as a control freak and as demanding. Because life is not perfect, you feel a continual sense of anger, resentment, and irritation because things are not going your way. Your life is overly organized and overly structured. You tend to obsess about the details of tasks that you have to accomplish. At times you may become paralyzed with fear that you will not perform a task to your unrealistically high expectations. You have little tolerance for the imperfections of others. You have a constant "to do" list going that you never finish. Inwardly you feel inadequate and even fraudulent. To be acceptable you take on a "win at all costs" philosophy. You may impose your perfectionist standards on others, and they resent it. You fail to realize the simple truth that either perfection is an impossibility or everything is already perfect because God made it.

Positive Score

With a positive score you have a rational, reasonable attitude toward your performance. You are not exclusively focused on objectives and outcomes—you enjoy the process. You are accepting of the mistakes you make and the mistakes and flaws of others. You try hard at what you do, but then you let go. You realize intuitively that you cannot control things in life; you can only influence them. You enjoy your accomplishments. You do not give yourself a hard time. You are not overly self-critical or judgmental. You realize that the journey, not the destination, is the goal of life. You do not feel compelled to be or do anything.

V. Egocentricity

Negative Score

A negative score indicates that you see yourself as the center of the universe. You expect things always to go your way. You feel entitled to things—success, love, happiness, etc. A good deal of the time you feel frustrated, irritable, angry, or sad because things are not going your way and others are not meeting your needs. You feel overly responsible for what is going on around you. You tend to personalize problem situations. You tend to see yourself as the primary cause of problems at home or at work and you fail to see that problems usually have multiple causes. Because you are so self-focused, it is difficult for you to empathize with others and see their points of view. You tend to think you are right in most instances. You somehow feel that others should be aware of your special abilities and unique contributions and your feel affronted when you do not get the treatment from others that you feel you deserve.

Positive Score

A positive score indicates that you tend to go with the flow in life. You do not expect preferential treatment. You can be flexible and adaptable in dealing with life's obstacles and disappointments. When a problem arises at home or work, you do not automatically assume that you are the cause of it. Because of this you spare yourself a lot of aggravation and other negative feelings. You are considerate of others. You are able to see and understand their views and opinions on things, and you are tolerant of their ideas. You have a holistic view of life and are aware of your place in it.

VI. Drivenness

Negative Score

A negative score indicates you have a lot to prove in life. When you become involved in an activity or pursuit, you lose perspective, you lose balance, and you may have poor boundaries. You throw yourself into activities compulsively and often neglect your physical and mental health. You cannot relax. You are always on the move. Sadly, you often do not enjoy the activities you are involved in. You frantically pursue them. Your behavior exasperates others. You may be attracted to high-risk, high-sensation-seeking activities and you can become addicted to the adrenaline rush they provide. Psychologically you may be running from something. You feel an inward push. You are compelled. You do not have a sense of inner freedom. A big fear that something catastrophic will happen if you slow down haunts you. You may have significant inner pain, grief, loss, or anxiety that propels you and drives you to keep active.

Positive Score

A positive score indicates that you approach activities in a balanced fashion. You do not feel that you have to do anything. You do not feel pushed to prove anything. You are not running from pain and discomfort. You can work and play hard, but you can also relax and enjoy an activity. You are not addicted to excitement. You have nothing really to prove.

CONCLUSION

Completing this survey can help raise your level of awareness of maladaptive patterns of thinking and believing that can impede your recovery from addictions. As you progress in recovery you can return to the test and take it again and again to follow any changes in your thinking, attitudes, and belief as recovery unfolds.

Bibliography

Big Book, Alcoholics Anonymous. (2001). 4th Edition. New York: Alcoholics Anonymous World Services Inc.

Blotnick, S. (1984). *The Corporate Steeplechase: Predictable Crises in a Business Career.* New York: Facts on File.

Budilovsky, J. and Adamson, E. (2003). *Complete Idiot's Guide to Meditation.* Second Edition. Indianapolis, IA: Alpha Books.

Cooper, C. L. and Marshall, J. (1977). *Understanding Executive Stress.* New York: Petrocelli Books.

Cooper, C. L. and Payne, R. (1980). *Current Concerns in Occupation Stress.* New York: Wiley.

Davich, V. (1998). *The Best Guide to Meditation.* New York: St. Martin's.

Dillbeck, M. C. and Orme-Johnson, D. W. (1987). Physiological Differences Between Transcendental Meditation and Rest. *American Psychologist* 42, 879-881.

Fields, R. and Vandenbelt, R. (2003). *Understanding Personality Problems and Addiction.* Dual Diagnosis Series [Pamphlet]. Center City, MN: Hazelden Publishing and Educational Services.

Grieff, B. S. and Munter, P. K. (1980). *Executive Family and Organizational Life.* New York: New American Library.

Hazelden Foundation (1988). *Keep it Simple: Working the 12 Steps.* Center City, MN: Hazelden Publishing and Educational Services.

Jeving, R., Wilson, A. F., and Davidson, J. M. (1978). Adrenocortical Activity During Meditation. *Hormones and Behaviour* 10, 54-60.

Kets de Vries, M. F. R. and Miller, D. (1984). *The Neurotic Organization: Diagnosing and Changing Counter Productive Styles of Management.* San Franscisco: Jossey-Bass Publishers.

Levinson, H. (1964). *Emotional Health in the World of Work.* New York: Harper and Rowe.

Levinson, H. (1975). *Executive Stress.* New York: New American Library.

O'Connell, D. F. (1985). The R.E.S.T. Program (Reducing Employee Stress and Tension), unpublished manual, 65 pages.

O'Connell, D. F. (2003a). Addressing the Dilemma of Executive Addiction. *Addiction Professional,* May, 26-35.

O'Connell, D. F. (2003b). *Awakening the Spirit: A Guide to Developing a Spiritual Program in Addiction Recovery,* Baltimore, MD: Publish America.

O'Connell, D. F. and Alexander, C. N. (1994). *Self-Recovery: Treating Addictions Using Transcendental Meditation and Mahrishi Ayurveda.* Binghamton, NY: The Haworth Press.

Orme-Johnson, D. W. (1987). Medical Care Utilization and the Transcendental Meditation program. *Psychosomatic Medicine* 49, 493-507.

Speller, L. (1989). *Executives in Crisis: Recognizing and Managing the Alcoholic, Drug Addicted or Mentally Ill Executives.* San Francisco: Jossey-Bass Publishers.

Weinrieb, R. M. and O'Brien, C. P. (1993). Persistent Cognitive Deficits Attributed to Substance Abuse. *Neurologic Clinics* 11(3), 663-689.

Index

Page numbers followed by the letter "f" indicate figures.

Mistaken beliefs, 87-89. *See also*
    Beliefs, dysfunctional
Monastery life, 91-92
Mood swings, 181-182
Moods, understanding, 67-73
Morality, step four, 132-133

Negative emotion, 77-87
    addiction and, 159, 161, 162
    catastrophizing, 81
    emotional reasoning, 79-80
    identifying, 83-84
    jumping to conclusions, 80
    overgeneralizing, 80
    personalizing, 81
    recording, 85, 86
Negotiation, conflict management, 56
Nervous system, alcohol/drug use
    effect on, 47-49
Neurotheology, 139-140
Niluss (saint), 140
Normal guilt, 173-174

Obstacles, spirituality, 111-117
O'Connell Dysfunctional Attitude
    Survey (ODAS), 9, 189-202
Outsource, help, 4, 125
Overgeneralizing, 80

Participative management, 125
Passivity, denial, 156
Pathological shame, 174
Patterns of failure, recovery, 177-179
Pedestal professionals, 123-124
Perfectionism, *xi-xii*, 4, 12, 200-201
Performance, 4
Personal resources, recovery and, 22, 25
Personalizing, 81
PET scan, 14
Phase of independence, recovery, 36
Physical health, in recovery, 172-173
Physical recovery goals, setting, 5-6, 7
Physical sensations, feelings as, 67-68
Physiology, meditation and, 101-106,
    102f, 103f, 105f, 106f
Planning, recovery process, 2

Post–acute withdrawal, 183-185
Postponement, conflict management, 57
Posttraumatic growth, 164
Prayer, 14, 92. *See also* Meditation
    step eleven, 139-141
Predisposed, addiction, 43-44
Problem solvers, conflict resolution, 56
Profitability, 3
Protection, defense mechanism, 71
Psychological help, in recovery, 173
Psychological recovery goals, setting,
    6, 8-14
Pure consciousness, 101

Questionnaires
    conflict resolution styles, 61-62
    relapse competency, 38-41

Rationalizing, defense mechanism, 70,
    156
Reality stage, recovery, 36
Reasoning, emotional, 79-80
Recovery. *See also* Addictions treatment
    aches/pains, 183
    anxiety, 182
    basics, 187
    colds, 183
    conflict and. *See* Conflict
    cramping, 183
    and cravings, 180-181
    dysfunctional families, impact on,
        164-165, 166
    and emotional augmentation, 181
    failure, patterns of, 177-179
    and flashbacks, 182
    food cravings in, 182
    forgetfulness, 183
    guilt, 173-174
    infections, 183
    insomnia in, 181
    maintenance. *See* Relapse
    mood swings, 181-182
    physical health in, 172-173
    psychological help, 173
    and roles, family, 165, 167, 168
    and rules, family, 164-165
    and sexual dysfunction, 182-183

Order a copy of this book with this form or online at:
http://www.haworthpress.com/store/product.asp?sku=5485

MANAGING YOUR RECOVERY FROM ADDICTION
A Guide for Executives, Senior Managers, and Other Professionals

_____in hardbound at $44.95 (ISBN: 978-0-7890-2739-9)

_____in softbound at $24.95 (ISBN: 978-0-7890-2740-5)

206 pages • Includes illustrations

Or order online and use special offer code HEC25 in the shopping cart.

COST OF BOOKS_____

☐ **BILL ME LATER:** (Bill-me option is good on US/Canada/Mexico orders only; not good to jobbers, wholesalers, or subscription agencies.)

POSTAGE & HANDLING_____
(US: $4.00 for first book & $1.50 for each additional book)
(Outside US: $5.00 for first book & $2.00 for each additional book)

☐ Check here if billing address is different from shipping address and attach purchase order and billing address information.

Signature_____

SUBTOTAL_____

☐ **PAYMENT ENCLOSED: $_____**

IN CANADA: ADD 6% GST_____

☐ **PLEASE CHARGE TO MY CREDIT CARD.**

STATE TAX_____
(NJ, NY, OH, MN, CA, IL, IN, PA, & SD residents, add appropriate local sales tax)

☐ Visa ☐ MasterCard ☐ AmEx ☐ Discover
☐ Diner's Club ☐ Eurocard ☐ JCB

FINAL TOTAL_____
(If paying in Canadian funds, convert using the current exchange rate, UNESCO coupons welcome)

Account #_____

Exp. Date_____

Signature_____

Prices in US dollars and subject to change without notice.

NAME_____

INSTITUTION_____

ADDRESS_____

CITY_____

STATE/ZIP_____

COUNTRY_____ COUNTY (NY residents only)_____

TEL_____ FAX_____

E-MAIL_____

May we use your e-mail address for confirmations and other types of information? ☐ Yes ☐ No
We appreciate receiving your e-mail address and fax number. Haworth would like to e-mail or fax special discount offers to you, as a preferred customer. **We will never share, rent, or exchange your e-mail address or fax number.** We regard such actions as an invasion of your privacy.

Order From Your Local Bookstore or Directly From
The Haworth Press, Inc.
10 Alice Street, Binghamton, New York 13904-1580 • USA
TELEPHONE: 1-800-HAWORTH (1-800-429-6784) / Outside US/Canada: (607) 722-5857
FAX: 1-800-895-0582 / Outside US/Canada: (607) 771-0012
E-mail to: orders@haworthpress.com

For orders outside US and Canada, you may wish to order through your local
sales representative, distributor, or bookseller.
For information, see http://haworthpress.com/distributors

(Discounts are available for individual orders in US and Canada only, not booksellers/distributors.)

PLEASE PHOTOCOPY THIS FORM FOR YOUR PERSONAL USE.
http://www.HaworthPress.com   BOF07

Dear Customer:

Please fill out & return this form to receive special deals & publishing opportunities for you! These include:

- availability of new books in your local bookstore or online
- one-time prepublication discounts
- free or heavily discounted related titles
- free samples of related Haworth Press periodicals
- publishing opportunities in our periodicals or Book Division

❑ OK! Please keep me on your regular mailing list and/or e-mailing list for new announcements!

Name _____

Address_____

STAPLE OR TAPE YOUR BUSINESS CARD HERE!

_____

*E-mail address _____
*Your e-mail address will never be rented, shared, exchanged, sold, or divested. You may "opt-out" at any time.
May we use your e-mail address for confirmations and other types of information? ❑ Yes ❑ No

Special needs:
Describe below any special information you would like:

- Forthcoming professional/textbooks
- New popular books
- Publishing opportunities in academic periodicals
- Free samples of periodicals in my area(s)

Special needs/Special areas of interest:

_____

_____

_____

_____

Please contact me as soon as possible. I have a special requirement/project:

_____

_____

_____

The Haworth Press Inc.

PLEASE COMPLETE THE FORM ABOVE AND MAIL TO:
Donna Barnes, Marketing Dept., The Haworth Press, Inc.
10 Alice Street, Binghamton, NY 13904–1580 USA
Tel: 1–800–429–6784 • Outside US/Canada Tel: (607) 722–5857
Fax: 1–800–895–0582 • Outside US/Canada Fax: (607) 771–0012
E-mail: orders@HaworthPress.com

GBIC07